Religions and Religious Movements

BUDDHISM

Other books in the Religions and
Religious Movements series:

Christianity
Confucianism
Hinduism
Islam
Judaism

Religions and Religious Movements
BUDDHISM

Jeff Hay, Book Editor

Bruce Glassman, Vice President

Bonnie Szumski, Publisher, Series Editor

Helen Cothran, Managing Editor

GREENHAVEN PRESS
An imprint of Thomson Gale, a part of The Thomson Corporation

Detroit • New York • San Francisco • San Diego • New Haven, Conn.
Waterville, Maine • London • Munich

THOMSON
━━━━━━━✦━━━━━━━ ™
GALE

LIBRARY OF CONGRESS CATALOGING-IN-PUBLICATION DATA

Buddhism / Jeff Hay, book editor.
    p. cm. — (Religions and religious movements)
    Includes bibliographical references and index.
    ISBN 0-7377-2563-X (lib. : alk. paper)
    1. Buddhism. I. Hay, Jeff. II. History of religions and religious movements.
BQ4055.B8513 2006
294.3—dc22
                                           2005046381

Contents

ings, including the notion that earthly behavior resulted in consequences known as karma, which might be good or bad. Bad karma led one further away from enlightenment.

6. The Spread of Buddhism 61

by Christmas Humphreys
Over many centuries, Buddhism spread from India to become the predominant religion of much of east Asia and Southeast Asia, where it subdivided into many sects and meshed with other religious and philosophical practices.

Chapter 2: The Smaller Path: Theravada Buddhism in Southeast Asia

1. Buddhism and Kingship in Sri Lanka 76

by Trevor Ling
Buddhist kings in Sri Lanka, an island off the Indian coast, try to maintain both the purity of the original Buddha's teachings and the example of Ashoka.

2. The Buddhist Calendar and Daily Life 85

by Robert C. Lester
In Burma, Thailand, Laos, and Cambodia, Buddhist practices are closely intertwined with beliefs in local spirits as well as the agricultural year, and believers emphasize merit making as a way to acquire good karma.

3. Becoming a Monk 95

by Donald K. Swearer
Many Theravada Buddhist men serve as monks for at least a short period of their lives. Monkhood serves as an important rite of passage.

4. An Outsider's Observations of Buddhist Life in Burma 105

by Norma Bixler
Burmese Buddhist practices are closely connected to personal needs and preferences, and monks play a central role in not only religion but the social order as well.

Chapter 3: The Greater Path: Mahayana Buddhism in East Asia

Chapter 4: Buddhism Around the World and in Modern Times

Foreword

"Religion is not what is grasped by the brain, but a heart grasp."
—Mohandas Gandhi, 1956

The impulse toward religion—to move beyond the world as we know it and ponder the larger questions of why we are here, whether there is a God who directs our lives, and how we should live—seems as universally human as breathing.

Yet, although this impulse is universal, different religions and their adherents are often at odds due to conflicts that stem from their opposing belief systems. These conflicts can also occur because many people have only the most tentative understanding of religions other than their own. In a time when religion seems to be at the root of growing tensions around the world, its study seems particularly relevant.

We live in a religiously diverse world. And while the world's many religions have coexisted for millennia, only recently, with information shared so easily and travel to even the most remote regions made possible for larger numbers of people, has this fact been fully acknowledged. It is no longer possible to ignore other religions, regardless of whether one views these religions positively or negatively.

The study of religion has also changed a great deal in recent times. Just a few decades ago in the United States, few students were exposed to any religion other than Christianity. Today, the study of religion reflects the pluralism of American society and the world at large. Religion courses and even current events classes focus on non-Christian religions as well as the religious experiences of groups that have in the past been marginalized by traditional Christianity, such as women and racial minorities.

In fact, the study of religion has been integrated into many different types of classes and disciplines. Anthropology, psychology, sociology, history, philosophy, political science, economics, and other fields often include discussions about different nations' religions and beliefs.

The study of religion involves so many disciplines because, for many cultures, it is integrated into many different parts of life. This point is often highlighted when American companies conduct business deals in Middle Eastern countries and inadvertently offend a host country's religious constrictions, for example. On both a small scale, such as personal travel, and on a large scale, such as international trade and politics, an understanding of the world's religions has become essential.

The goals of the Religions and Religious Movements series are several. The first is to provide students a historical context for each of the world's religions. Each book focuses on one religion and explores, through primary and secondary sources, its fundamental belief system, religious works of importance, and prominent figures. By using articles from a variety of sources, each book provides students with different theological and historical contexts for the religion.

The second goal of the series is to explore the challenges that each religion faces today. All of these religions are experiencing challenges and changes—some theological, some political—that are forcing alterations in attitude and belief. By reading about these current dilemmas, students will come to understand that religions are not abstract concepts, but a vital part of peoples' lives.

The last and perhaps most important objective is to make students aware of the wide variety of religious beliefs, as well as the factors, common to all religions. Every religion attempts to puzzle out essential questions as well as provide a model for doing good in the world. By using the books in the Religions and Religious Movements series, students will find that people with divergent, closely held beliefs may learn to live together and work toward the same goals.

Introduction

Buddhism is a religion with no gods. Unlike Hindus, in whose religion Buddhism finds its origins, Buddhists worship no complex and picturesque collection of deities. They also see no attraction in the paternalistic, merciful, yet judgmental god offered by the three major monotheistic religions: Judaism, Christianity, and Islam. Instead, Buddhists hold forth the possibility of individual enlightenment, of eternal peace, of a sense of oneness with the universe and creation. They call this goal nirvana.

Historically, Buddhists have differed broadly on the different ways by which people might reach nirvana. There are two major schools of Buddhism, the Theravada path of Sri Lanka and Southeast Asia and the Mahayana path of China, Japan, Korea, Vietnam, and Tibet. But even within those schools there are numerous sects and approaches. Buddhism, indeed, has been a very flexible faith, adjusting itself to suit the habits and histories of the countries where it has taken hold. This flexibility has continued as Buddhism has spread outside Asia to be a truly global faith with adherents on all continents. Many of the adherents are Asian immigrants to Europe, North America, or Australia, but others are local people who have adopted a Buddhist path in preference to either the religions they grew up with or the secularism of the modern industrialized world.

They are testimony to the richness and vitality of this ancient faith and its continuing appeal around the world.

Buddhism emerged from ancient India in the fifth century B.C. when the local religion, Hinduism, was taking shape. Among the Hindu ideas that Buddhists were to adopt were the notion of reincarnation, in which the soul is reborn lifetime after lifetime in new bodies, and the belief in karma, or the consequence of action. Buddhists also took up the concept of dharma, a term with several meanings that include "duty," "law," and "path." Most fundamentally, Buddhists, like Hindus, believe that the universe is one, that all life is connected. Nevertheless, Buddhism modified these adopted notions to suit a new vision that promised a way to end what both see as the largest feature of human existence: suffering. Hindu thinking, generally, argues that one should accept suffering as the price for misdeeds in earlier lifetimes, for an accumulation of bad karma. But Buddhism, from the beginning, thought otherwise.

Buddhism's Indian Origins

Stories abound about Siddhartha Gautama, the founder of Buddhism also known as Sakyamuni, the sage of the Sakyas (his tribal clan). The outline of his life story, as described in the canon of classical Buddhist texts written down in the first century B.C., also serves as the story of the origins of the faith. Siddhartha was born in the sixth or fifth century B.C. (scholarly opinions differ) in a small kingdom in what is now either northern India or the nation of Nepal. His clan, the Sakyas, were the local rulers, members of the warrior caste of Hindu society. Siddhartha was raised to be a soldier and a king by his father, Suddhodana. He proved to be skilled in archery, horsemanship, diplomacy, and indeed all the arts of war and rulership, and as a young man he married Yasodhana, a princess from a neighboring kingdom.

Although Suddhodana tried to shelter Siddhartha from the darker aspects of life—sickness, sorrow, even aging—the young prince felt restricted by the comforts and pleasures of his palace. While in his late twenties he began to make visits to a nearby city. The things he saw there convinced him that suffering was the great problem of human existence. Siddhartha was particularly struck by an aging man, a sick beggar, and a funeral procession, clear signs to him of the sureness of suffering and death. Inspired by the sight of a Hindu ascetic (a holy man who had given up all possessions in favor of meditation and devotion), the prince gave up his kingdom, his princess, and their newborn baby. He pledged to find the source of suffering and to see if there might be some way to lessen it or overcome it.

After spending some time with a group of Hindu ascetics, Siddhartha rejected their path of worldly denial for its lack of common sense and because it seemed to offer no answer to the problem of suffering. Somewhat frustrated, he chose a spot on a riverside near the northern Indian town of Bodh-Gaya, where he would remain until he attained the enlightenment he was seeking. He sat down to meditate under a bodhi tree. There, he went through emotions ranging from loneliness to lust as well as the bitter pangs of memory and self-doubt. He was challenged by Mara, a tempter often depicted in Buddhist mythology as a god of death, to return to his life of luxury, power, and earthly attachments. He saw visions of his soul's past lives and was reminded of the impermanence of all things, of the transitory nature of life. Finally, Siddhartha received the answers he was looking for: that life, indeed, is suffering but that suffering can be overcome. In so doing he advanced from being a bodhisattva, the "little Buddha" he had been prophesied to be as an infant, to a full Buddha, an enlightened one. He had achieved nirvana.

The Buddha's Enlightenment and First Teachings

After making his way to Sarnath, a village outside the ancient and holy Hindu city of Benares (Varanasi), the Buddha preached his first sermons to a small group of followers who were impressed by both his sense of peace and his authoritative presence. In these lessons he introduced the ideas that would be fundamental to virtually all later forms of Buddhism. These were the four noble truths: Suffering is the essential fact of human existence; suffering is caused by desire (i.e., an excessive desire for personal satisfaction); suffering can be overcome by doing away with desire; and finally, the proper way to achieve this is to follow the eightfold path. The eight characteristics that make up this path are right views, right thinking, right speech, right action, right way of life, right endeavor, right mindfulness, and right meditation. The Buddha also preached that it was essential for those seeking enlightenment to follow a middle way during life, to avoid extremes of either asceticism or personal indulgence. These ideas were to be the foundation of the Buddhist dharma, or path.

After the original group of followers had grown to number sixty or so, the Buddha told them to spread the message of his path to enlightenment. These disciples formed the first Sangha, or Buddhist community, and were to learn by experience that it was easiest to follow the eightfold path and live according to the middle way if they became monks, devoting themselves to achieving enlightenment and teaching others their practices. The Buddha taught them a simple motto for new converts:

> I take my refuge in the Buddha
> I take my refuge in the Dharma
> I take my refuge in the Sangha.

It is still repeated by many Buddhists today, and the emphasis on monks and monasteries was to be a central part of virtually every variation of Buddhism. Indeed, Buddhism is a religion of monks rather than priests or scholars. One can choose to be a monk for life or simply enter a monastery for a short period of time. Even women can enter monasteries, although they generally have to accept a status subordinate to that of men as well as physical separation, and their roles in monastic orders are highly influenced by local custom and tradition. Nevertheless, the original Buddha accepted the notion that women, too, could become enlightened.

The Buddha himself, meanwhile, continued to preach his message, attracting new converts and the patronage of a few wealthy men, until he died at the age of eighty. Among his last words was a reminder that, despite his growing reknown and the popularity of his teachings, he was no savior. He was just a man who had suggested a path; whether or not a person achieved enlightenment, or even moved in that direction, was ultimately his or her own responsibility.

Buddhism remained a fairly small faith for two centuries after the Buddha's death. When an Indian emperor by the name of Ashoka adopted Buddhist principles, however, it achieved widespread fame, attracted thousands of new converts, and began to spread outside India. Ashoka was the third emperor of the Mauryan dynasty, which ruled India from 321 B.C. until 185 B.C.; his grandfather, Chandragupta, had faced down the Greek armies of Alexander the Great in northwestern India around 325 B.C. When he took the throne in 273 B.C. Ashoka was a warrior king like Chandragupta and his father, Bindusara. But after the conquest of the recalcitrant kingdom of Kalinga in a series of battles that left tens of thousands dead, he adopted many of the ideas of Buddhism, saddened by the violence and destruction of war. For the rest of his reign he tried to govern according to the principle of ahimsa, nonviolence, rejecting even such practices as meat eating and hunting. He urged his citizens to do the same. Across his realm he constructed some five thousand pillars on which were inscribed both Ashoka's own story of conversion and Buddhist guidelines for daily living; thirty-seven of these "rock edicts" still stand.

Thanks to an Emperor, Buddhism Expands

Ashoka also strengthened Buddhism and encouraged it to spread by building dozens of memorial mounds known as stupas, giving grants of land (and therefore wealth) to prominent monks and monasteries, and making pilgrimages to holy sites. He encouraged government officials to do likewise, and required them to spend time enforcing codes of morality and behavior. Ashoka even provided early forms of public welfare, such as hospitals, rest houses for travelers, and schools for women, all of which were quite unusual for his era.

In addition to developing these institutions, which helped turn Buddhism into an "organized" religion, Ashoka tried to spread Buddhism outside of India, using

The Spread of Buddhism

his status as one of the world's great emperors to lend prestige to the effort. He sent Buddhist missionaries and envoys to regions as far away as Egypt and Greece to the west and Burma to the east. It was in the nearby island kingdom of Sri Lanka (formerly Ceylon), however, that Ashoka's missionary efforts reached their greatest fruition. After Ashoka's death in 232 B.C. and the return of India to Hindu predominance, Sri Lanka became the center of Buddhist development and the base for its further expansion into Southeast Asia. Indeed, it was in Sri Lanka that many of the central Buddhist texts were finally written down in the first century B.C. Most notable among these were the Tripitaka, the "three baskets" of wisdom, one of which contains the Dhammapada, a collection of the Buddha's teachings.

The states of Southeast Asia, ranging from modern Myanmar (formerly Burma) to modern Indonesia, were for many centuries part of the cultural orbit of India, tied to the subcontinent by trade, dynastic connections, and religious ideas. In terms of religion these states have seen a sort of layering effect: As new religions have come along they have been grafted onto earlier beliefs and practices. This effect can be seen in such monuments as Borobodur on the Indonesian island of Java, which contains both Hindu and Buddhist elements preserved by a population that, after 1300, was mostly Islamic. It can also be seen in the ruins of the powerful Khmer Empire based in Cambodia (ca. 800–1250), the hybrid Hindu-Buddhist civilization that created Angkor Wat, one of the great historical monuments of all time. In those areas of Southeast Asia that remained predominantly Buddhist—Burma (Myanmar), Thailand, Cambodia, and Laos—believers maintain the form of Buddhism originally developed in India and Sri Lanka.

Theravada Buddhism

This form of Buddhism is known as Theravada Buddhism, "the teaching of the elders." Theravada Buddhism is generally accepted to be much closer to the kind of Buddhism practiced by the first monastic orders than the open, diverse Mahayana Buddhism of China, Korea, and Japan. Theravada is centered around monks and temples. The monks themselves continue to strive to live according to Buddhist precepts: shaving their heads, wearing saffron-colored robes, and refusing to eat after noon. And in Theravada countries it is normal for young men to serve as monks for a period of time. Temples, meanwhile, are centers of both education and community life. For laypeople, much of the emphasis of Theravada devotion is on merit making, or doing good works in order to build up karma and advance toward nirvana. Common forms of merit making include donating money to temples and providing for monks. In fact, a common sight in Theravada countries is the early morning parades of groups of monks walking through the streets holding begging bowls into which local women put rice and other food. The monks do not need to beg; the ritual simply provides laypeople with an opportunity to make merit by showing their generosity.

Theravada Buddhism retains certain elements, however, of the hybrid nature of religious practice in Southeast Asia. Many believers worship the original Buddha as a "perfected being," almost a god, a practice that was specifically warned against by the founder. In many cases they also continue to believe in and worship the nature spirits that predated the arrival of Buddhism. In Thailand, for instance, every home and building contains a "spirit house" where people place offerings to propitiate these spirits in order to guard against ill fortune and ensure good luck.

As in much of Southeast Asia, Buddhism arrived in China by way of itinerant monks, and just as Sri Lanka served as the base for the expansion of Theravada Buddhism, China was the base for the popularization of Mahayana Buddhism, the "greater path." In the centuries after the fall of the Han dynasty (A.D. 220), an era of outside invasion and political and social chaos, many Chinese turned toward Buddhism as an alternative to Confucianism, the worldly philosophy of the nation's traditional and now discredited elites. By the fourth and fifth centuries, Buddhism was strong in China. And over the next centuries, numerous Buddhist sects arose and their teachings, like much else in Chinese culture, took root in the Chinese orbit of civilization: Korea, Japan, and Vietnam. It is in these areas where Mahayana Buddhism has had its greatest flowering.

Mahayana Buddhism

Mahayana Buddhism emerged in India in the second and first centuries B.C. when certain monastic orders and kings transformed the image of the Buddha from that of an ordinary man who had shown a path to enlightenment to a figure who, in and of himself, was worthy of great devotion. They claimed that over the course of many lifetimes he had become perfect and had returned to earth from the *Tushita* heaven, a conception of an otherworld that does not exist in more orthodox forms of Buddhism except as a metaphor. Since the Buddha had achieved perfection and had traveled between heaven and earth, Mahayana thinkers argued, it was logical that other figures could do the same. Mahayana Buddhism is populated with some of these other figures. They are described as "little Buddhas," or *bodhisattvas*, and they function as objects of reverence and devotion in ways similar to the gods of other faiths.

The people of China found Mahayana teachings congenial since they seemed flexible enough to incorporate such Chinese traditions as filial piety and the emphasis on rituals as a reminder of one's place in the divine order. Moreover, Mahayana Buddhism offered something to ordinary Chinese people that neither Confucianism nor the other major stream of Chinese thought, Taoism, could: the comfort of looking forward to an afterlife. Confucianism had little to say about life after death, and Taoism, with its emphasis on aligning oneself with nature, was not concerned with such notions. But Mahayana teachings informed people that there was such a thing as a heaven to look forward to.

This conception is clearest in the Pure Land school of Buddhism, which took shape in China in the fifth century (although like almost all Buddhist schools, it had its earlier Indian advocates). Pure Land Buddhism is based on reverence for the Buddha Amitabha (O-mi-tuo in China, Amida in Japan and Korea), a legendary monk who in the far distant past rose to an advanced level of enlightenment and came to preside over a "land of bliss," the so-called western paradise. Amitabha offers even more than Gautama Buddha: not merely enlightenment and understanding but purity and bliss in a "Buddha land" where one can truly follow the dharma without the distractions of life on earth. He demonstrates his generosity by transferring his own merit to believers, a task that is carried out by faith rather than through ritual. Pure Land Buddhism proved to be extremely popular among ordinary people throughout east Asia.

Many Pure Land Buddhists find in the bodhisattva Kuan Yin an even more congenial figure than Amitabha. Kuan Yin is the Chinese version of the Indian bodhisattva Avalokiteshvara. Through a mysterious process unknown to experts, the masculine Avalokiteshvara was transformed into the feminine, maternal Kuan Yin, "goddess" of mercy across east Asia. In either form the bodhisattva is one of generosity and protection, shielding people from harm, averting disease and disaster, and even granting children or other boons to those who want them. In Pure Land mythology Kuan Yin is often described as striding the waves or riding on a cloud, and it is she who transports believers to the western paradise presided over by Amitabha.

Pure Land and Zen Buddhism

Somewhat less popular than the Pure Land school, due to their strict emphasis on individual effort, were the so-called meditative schools of Mahayana Buddhism, which also arose in China around the fifth and sixth centuries. The most influential of these was the Ch'an school, which is better known by its Japanese name, Zen. Supposedly founded by an Indian monk named Bodhidharma, who settled in southern China in the sixth century, Zen Buddhism rejects the emphasis on accumulating merit that other schools recommend. Instead, the Zen school argues that true enlightenment can be found only by looking within oneself. Sacred texts, merit-making exercises, even the performing of rituals often only get in the way of this effort. Those seeking the Zen path should, instead, accept the verbal, one-to-one teachings of masters and examine their own nature, a process best achieved through meditation. The goal was to open oneself up to flashes of insight about the true nature of the self and of the universe. These "awakenings," *satori* in Japanese, were in and of themselves transformative, and they were signs that one was approaching the status of Zen master, or even Buddhahood itself.

Although it remained a part of Chinese Buddhism, Zen truly came into its own in Japan. Several Zen schools rose to importance there, but the largest were the Soto and Rinzai sects, both of which emerged in the twelfth century (although similar, earlier versions existed in China and Korea). Established by a monk named Dogen, Soto Zen emphasizes individual meditation called, simply, *zazen*, or "sitting meditation." Dogen taught that through this means one could avoid distractions, everything from monastic disputes to excessive thinking about obscure and irrelevant things. Rinzai Zen, on the other hand, offers meditation on riddles or puzzles known as koan. One famous koan asks, "What is the sound of one hand clapping?" Both forms of Zen took firm hold in Japan, often with the support of wealthy men or emperors, and Japan became dotted with Zen monasteries where people could practice meditation. However, Zen remained mostly a pursuit of elites or self-selected misfits. Most ordinary Japanese continued to follow one of the various branches of Pure Land Buddhism with its friendly bodhisattvas, or Shinto, the native religion.

Zen in Japan, and to a lesser extent in China, Korea, and Vietnam, also allowed for the appreciation and cultivation of earthly life rather than the rejection of it, which, at first glance, appears common to most Buddhist schools. Zen Buddhists believe that all experience can be tuned to the "awakening" of immediate insight, even archery and swordsmanship; one demonstration of Zen capability was to perform successfully without being concerned about the outcome of the efforts (i.e., to win without caring if you won). Zen artists and writers, meanwhile, produced some of the greatest works in Chinese and Japanese painting and poetry. Even the drinking of tea, as practiced in the traditional Japanese tea ceremony developed in the sixteenth century, could help one experience a moment of enlightenment.

Tibet's Distinct Brand of Buddhism

Tantric Buddhism, a very different branch of the Mahayana school, took hold in Tibet and other regions in northern and central Asia. Tantric Buddhism was highly influenced by the tantric school of Hinduism, which emphasized strange rituals, symbols, and elaborate and sometimes mysterious ceremonies as means to achieve one's religious goals. Tantric Buddhism added to these characteristics a focus on monks and temples and the attempt to reconcile opposing forces in pursuit of the dharma. It came to Tibet, an isolated region of mountains and high desert plains north of India, in the seventh and eighth centuries B.C., and evolved over the next centuries. Thanks to Tibet's isolation, further influences from India or China were slow in coming, and therefore this distinct version of Buddhism was free to evolve in its own way, often incorporating earlier beliefs such as divine kingship. In addition to Tibet, other regions that adopted Tantric Buddhism include the Himalayan mountain kingdom of Bhutan and the central and northern Asian areas of Mongolia. It also influenced Buddhist practice in northern India and Nepal, although Buddhism in these regions was constricted by both Hindu hegemony and the Muslim conquests of much of India beginning in the eleventh century.

The dominant form of Tibetan Buddhism came to be known as "Yellow Hat" Buddhism because of the caps worn by believers. It was presided over by large communities of monks, who in Tibet are called lamas, or "superior ones." In the sixteenth century the Yellow Hats began to refer to their leader as the Dalai Lama, which roughly translates as "ocean of wisdom" lama. The title of Dalai Lama, Tibetans believe, is passed down via reincarnation, each subsequent Dalai Lama being a reincarnation of the previous one. Dalai Lamas are also held to be reincarnations of the bodhisattva Avalokiteshvara. In the seventeenth century the fifth Dalai Lama established himself as the political as well as spiritual leader of Tibet, reigning from the ancient

Potala Palace in Lhasa, the Tibetan capital, to represent this dual role.

The current Dalai Lama, the fourteenth, is probably the world's most famous Buddhist. He went into exile in 1959 when the Communist Chinese, who had invaded and taken over Tibet in 1951, violently put down a nationalist uprising. During this violent year, thousands of Tibetan monks were killed and hundreds of temples desecrated or destroyed. After leaving, the Dalai Lama set up a residence in Dharamsala in northern India. His status as a political leader in exile, as well as his generosity and charm, have made him famous around the world. He speaks frequently to large audiences and has appeared as the subject of many books and films. Aware that he might never return to his homeland, and concerned that Tibetan Buddhism might die out in the face of the dual onslaughts of the Chinese occupation on the one hand and technological and economic modernization on the other, the Dalai Lama has taken great efforts to preserve the tradition. His writings and lessons are extensive, and Buddhist monasteries have been built in a number of countries. Meanwhile, many celebrities and other prominent people have voiced support for both Tibetan Buddhism and the cause of Tibetan independence.

Buddhism Around the World

The Dalai Lama's fame is only one sign of Buddhism's current status as a global religion. Asian immigrants have brought Buddhism to their new countries, and the United States, Canada, Great Britain, Australia, and other Western nations have large and diverse Buddhist communities. Los Angeles alone has distinct Chinese,

Japanese, Vietnamese, Korean, Cambodian, Thai, Sri Lankan, and Tibetan Buddhist centers. Buddhism has also been reintroduced on a large scale into India, the land of its birth. And like the Dalai Lama himself, some Buddhists have found themselves embroiled in political and social turmoil. A notable example was the movement among Vietnamese Buddhists to help end the long war in their country that lasted, in all its manifestations, from 1946 to 1975. Vietnamese monks protested not only the war itself but the corruption of the South Vietnamese government and its attacks on their orders. Indeed, one of the most famous photographs from the Vietnam War is of a monk who, as a form of public protest and with the support of fellow believers, doused himself with gasoline and burned himself to death at a busy intersection in Saigon, South Vietnam's capital.

In the twentieth century, Buddhism became attractive to large numbers of Westerners as well. Contact between Buddhists and Westerners dates back to the first few centuries B.C., when there were Greek-speaking Buddhists in the lands stretching from India westward to the Mediterranean Sea, and European merchants and explorers certainly encountered Buddhism during their Asian journeys from the time of Marco Polo in the thirteenth century onward. But it was not until the late 1800s, when a religious movement known as theosophy arose, that Buddhist ideas began to become familiar in Europe and the United States. Theosophists borrowed many ideas from Buddhism, and its founders, Helena Blavatsky and H.S. Olcott, traveled to India to seek the source of these ideas. They went on to set up study centers in both the United States and Great Britain, one of the longest lasting of which was located in San Diego's Point Loma area.

It was Zen Buddhism, however, that had the greatest attraction to Western followers. Zen masters, most notably a Japanese monk named D.T. Suzuki, began to set up Zen societies on the U.S. West Coast and in New York City in the 1920s. They in turn influenced Englishmen and Americans like Christmas Humphreys and Alan Watts, both prominent in the 1940s and 1950s, to adopt Buddhism and explain it using Western frames of reference. Watts, in particular, argued that Zen offered a satisfying alternative to both the judgmentalism and guilt of Christianity and Judaism and the empty materialism of modern Western life. These influences even trickled down into popular culture, and a kind of simplified Zen can be found in the writings of such 1950s writers as Jack Kerouac and Alan Ginsberg. Zen, or at least a westernized version of it, went on to become a part of the American counterculture that established itself in the 1960s, and it has established permanent institutions. Notable among these are the large Zen Center of Los Angeles and the Zen Mission Society near Mount Shasta in northern California.

Regardless of where they live, Buddhists follow their own calendar, beginning with the year of Gautama Buddha's enlightenment. For them the year 2004 is the year 2547. But they do not take the designation too seriously, remaining quite comfortable with other dating systems and with other cultures and ways of life. For they have learned, by finding refuge in the Buddha, the dharma, and the Sangha, that detachment from desire and from worldly things is the best way to achieve peace of mind in a troubled, diverse world.

CHAPTER 1

The Origins of Buddhism

Basic Buddhist Beliefs

by Burton Watson

The following selection provides a basic introduction to the origins of Buddhism and its central beliefs. Its author is religious scholar Burton Watson, and it is taken from the introduction to his translation, from a Chinese source, of the Lotus Sutra, an important Buddhist text especially revered in east Asia. Buddhism grew ever more complex as it expanded across south and east Asia from its origins in sixth- or fifth-century-B.C. India, producing numerous schools and sects and often blending with earlier, local beliefs such as faith in nature spirits or reverence for ancestors. Nevertheless, most Buddhists hold to the basic tenets that Watson summarizes here. These include the four noble truths, concerned with overcoming suffering, and the eight-fold path, which provides a set of general moral guidelines. The ultimate goal for the individual in Buddhism is to achieve enlightenment or Buddhahood, and in so doing leave the cycle of reincarnation and enter the state of being known as nirvana. Burton Watson has translated many Buddhist texts from Chinese and Japanese into English, including *Ryokan: Zen Monk-Poet of Japan* and *Selected Writings of Nichiren*.

Burton Watson, trans., *The Lotus Sutra*. New York: Columbia University Press, 1993. Copyright © 1993 by Columbia University Press, 61 W. Sixty-second St., New York, NY 10023. All rights reserved. Reproduced by permission.

Gautama, or Shakyamuni Buddha, the founder of Buddhism, appears to have lived in India sometime around the sixth or fifth century BC. Though it is difficult to describe his doctrines in detail, Buddhologists customarily accept several formulas as representative of his teachings. Most famous of these are the so-called four noble truths. These teach that (1) all existence in the *saha* world, the world in which we live at present, is marked by suffering; (2) that suffering is caused by craving; (3) that by doing away with craving one can gain release from suffering and reach a state of peace and enlightenment, often called nirvana; (4) that there is a method for achieving this goal, namely, the discipline known as the eightfold path. This is a set of moral principles enjoining one to cultivate right views, right thinking, right speech, right action, right way of life, right endeavor, right mindfulness, and right meditation.

Another doctrine is that of the twelve-linked chain of causation or dependent origination, which illustrates step by step the causal relationship between ignorance and suffering. The purpose of the doctrine, like that of the four noble truths, is to wake one to the true nature of reality and help one to achieve emancipation from ignorance and suffering.

In order to pursue the kind of strenuous discipline needed to gain such release, it was thought all but imperative that one leave secular life and become a member of the Buddhist Order, which consisted of both monks and nuns. There, free from family entanglements and worldly concerns, one could devote oneself to a life of poverty, celibacy, and religious study and discipline, supported by the alms of the lay community. Lay believers could acquire religious merit by assisting the Order, observing the appropriate rules of moral conduct, and carrying out devotional practices such as pay-ing obeisance at the stupas or memorial towers that housed the relics of the Buddha. But it was thought that they would have to wait until future existences before they could hope to gain full release from suffering.

Karma and Reincarnation

Buddhism, it should be noted, took over from earlier Indian thought the belief in karma. According to this belief, all a person's moral actions, whether good or bad, produce definite effects in the person's life, though such effects may take some time before mani-festing themselves. According to the Indian view, living beings pass through an endless cycle of death and re-birth, and the ill effects of an evil action in one life may not become evident until some future existence; but that they will appear eventually is inescapable. Hence only by striving to do good in one's present existence can one hope to escape even greater suffering in a fu-ture life.

Buddhism vehemently denied that there is any indi-vidual soul or personal identity that passes over from one existence to the next—to suppose there is is simply to open the way for further craving—but it did accept the idea of rebirth or transmigration, and taught that the circumstances or realm into which a being is reborn are determined by the good or bad acts done by that being in previous existences. This meant, among other things, that one did not necessarily have to struggle for release from suffering within a single lifetime, but could work at the goal of salvation step by step, per-forming good moral and devotional acts that would in-sure one of rebirth in more favorable circumstances in the future, and in this way gradually raising one's level of spiritual attainment.

The tenets and practices of the religion I have described above are often referred to as Hinayana Buddhism. But Hinayana, which means "Lesser Vehicle," is a derogatory term, applied to early Buddhism by a group within the religion that called itself Mahayana or the "Great Vehicle" and represented its doctrines as superior to and superseding those of earlier Buddhism. In keeping with the spirit of religious tolerance and mutual understanding that prevails in most quarters today, writers usually try to avoid use of the term, "Hinayana," instead referring to the earlier form of Buddhism as "Theravada" or "The Teachings of the Elders," which is the name used by the branch of it that continues in existence today. This is the form of Buddhism that prevails at present in Sri Lanka, Burma, Thailand, Cambodia, and Laos.

Buddhism's Two Major Forms

The Mahayana movement appears to have begun in India around the first or second century of the Common Era [the first and second centuries A.D.]. In part it was probably a reaction against the great emphasis upon monastic life that marked earlier Buddhism and against the arid psychological and metaphysical speculations that characterize much of early Buddhist philosophy. It aimed to open up the religious life to a wider proportion of the population, to accord a more important role to lay believers, to give more appealing expression to the teachings and make them more readily accessible.

In earlier Buddhism the goal of religious striving had been to achieve the state of arhat or "worthy," one who has "nothing more to learn" and has escaped rebirth in the lower realms of existence. Even to reach this state, however, it was believed, required many lifetimes of strenuous exertion. But Mahayana urged men and women to aim for nothing less than the achievement of the highest level of enlightenment, that of Buddhahood. Enormous help in reaching this exalted goal, it was stressed, would come to them through figures known as bodhisattvas, beings who are dedicated not only to attaining enlightenment for themselves but, out of their immense compassion, to helping others to do likewise. Earlier Buddhism often described Shakyamuni Buddha as a bodhisattva in his previous existences, when he was still advancing toward enlightenment. But in Mahayana texts such as the Lotus Sutra the bodhisattvas are pictured as unlimited in number, all-seeing and all-caring, capable of extending boundless aid and succor to those who call upon them in sincere faith. Indeed, this great emphasis upon the role of the bodhisattva is one of the main characteristics that distinguish Mahayana thought from that of earlier Buddhism.

At first the proponents of these new Mahayana beliefs seem in many cases to have lived side by side in the same monasteries as the adherents of the earlier teachings, their religious practice centering around the worship of the Buddha's relics housed in the stupas or memorial towers. But doctrinal clashes arose from time to time and the two groups eventually drew apart. The Mahayana doctrines appear to have dominated in northwestern India, where they spread into the lands of Central Asia and thence into China. As a result, Chinese Buddhism was from the first overwhelmingly Mahayana in character, and it was this Mahayana version of the faith that in time was introduced to Korea, Japan, and Vietnam, where it continues in existence today.

The Original Buddha Finds Enlightenment

by Elizabeth Lyons and Heather Peters

The founder of Buddhism was Siddhartha Gautama, who was also known as Sakyamuni, or the "sage" of his tribe, the Sakyas. Born in the northern Indian region above the River Ganges in the sixth century B.C., the original Buddha, or enlightened one, was a member of the Hindu Kshatriya, or warrior caste. After forsaking his kingly destiny and embarking upon a spiritual search, Siddhartha passed through a series of trials, temptations, and meditations until he achieved enlightenment by realizing that humankind was burdened by suffering and ignorance and that there were ways to overcome both these burdens.

In the following selection, Elizabeth Lyons and Heather Peters describe how Siddhartha achieved enlightenment and began to teach his discoveries to a small group of disciples, retelling a story now known to hundreds of millions of Buddhists worldwide. Lyons and Peters are experts in Buddhist and religious art who served as cocurators of the exhibit of Buddhist art at the University Museum at the University of Pennsylvania.

One night Mahamaya, chief queen of Suddhodhana, king of the Sakyas, dreamt that she was carried away to the divine lake Anavatapta in the Himalayas, where she was bathed by the heavenly guardians of the four quarters of the universe. A great white elephant holding a lotus flower in his trunk approached her, and entered her side. . . . Next day the dream was interpreted for her by wise men—she had conceived a wonderful son, who would be either a Universal Emperor . . . or a Universal Teacher. The child was born in a grove of sal trees called Lumbini, near the capital of the Sakyas, Kapilavastu, while his mother was on the way to her parents' home for her confinement. At birth he stood upright, took seven strides, and spoke: "This is my last birth—henceforth there is no more birth for me." The boy was named Siddhartha, at a great ceremony on the fifth day from his birth. His *gotra* [clan] name was Gautama . . . by which he is commonly referred to in Buddhist literature. The soothsayers prophesied that he would become a Universal Emperor, with the exception of one, who declared that four signs would convince him of the misery of the world, and he would become a Universal Teacher. To prevent this prophecy coming true King Suddhodhana resolved that he should never know the sorrows of the world. He was reared in delightful palaces, from whose parks every sign of death, disease and misery was removed. He learned all the arts that a prince should learn, and excelled as a student. He married his cousin Yasodhara, whom he won at a great contest at which he performed feats of strength and skill. . . .

But for all his prosperity and success he was not inwardly happy, and for all the efforts of his father he did see the four signs foretold, which were to decide his career, for the gods knew his destiny, and it was they who placed the signs before him. One day, as he was driving round the royal park with his faithful charioteer Channa, he saw an aged man, in the last stages of infirmity and decrepitude—actually a god, who had taken this disguise in order that Siddhartha Gautama might become a Buddha. Siddhartha asked Channa who this repulsive being was, and when he learned that all men must grow old he was even more troubled in mind. This was the first sign. The second came a little later, in the same way, in the form of a very sick man, covered with boils and shivering with fever. The third was even more terrible—a corpse, being carried to the cremation-ground, followed by weeping mourners. But the fourth sign brought hope and consolation—a wandering religious beggar, clad in a simple yellow robe, peaceful and calm, with a mien of inward joy. On seeing him Siddhartha realized where his destiny lay, and set his heart on becoming a wanderer.

Hearing of this King Suddhodhana doubled his precautions. Siddhartha was made a virtual prisoner, though still surrounded with pleasures and luxuries of all kinds; his heart knew no peace, and he could never forget the four signs. One morning the news was brought to him that Yasodhara had given birth to a son, but it gave him no pleasure. That night there were great festivities, but when all were sleeping, he roused Channa, who saddled his favourite horse, Kanthaka, and he rode off into the night, surrounded by rejoicing demigods, who cushioned the fall of his horse's hoofs so that no one should hear his departure. . . .

When far from the city he stripped off his jewellery and fine garments and put on a hermit's robe, provided by an attendant demigod. . . . Thus Siddhartha performed his "Great Going Forth". . . . and became a wandering ascetic, owning nothing but the robe he wore.

At first, he begged his food as a wanderer, but he soon gave up this life for that of a forest hermit. From a sage named Alara Kalama he learned the technique of meditation, and the lore of Brahman as taught in the Upanisads [Hindu religious wisdom], but he was not convinced that man could obtain liberation from sorrow by self-discipline and knowledge, so he joined forces with five ascetics who were practising the most rigorous self-mortification in the hope of wearing away their karma and obtaining final bliss.

His penances became so severe that the five quickly recognised him as their leader. For six years he tortured himself until he was nothing but a walking skeleton. One day, worn out by penance and hunger, he fainted, and his followers believed that he was dead. But after a while he recovered consciousness, and realized that his fasts and penances had been useless. He again began to beg food, and his body regained its strength. The five disciples left him in disgust at his backsliding.

One day Siddhartha Gautama, now thirty-five years old, was seated beneath a large pipal tree on the outskirts of the town of Gaya, in the realm of Bimbisara, king of Magadha. Sujata, the daughter of a nearby farmer, brought him a large bowl of rice boiled in milk. After eating some of this he bathed, and that evening, again sitting beneath the pipal tree, he made a solemn vow that, though his bones wasted away and his blood dried up, he would not leave his seat until the riddle of suffering was solved.

So for forty-nine days he sat beneath the tree. At first he was surrounded by hosts of gods and spirits, awaiting the great moment of enlightenment; but they soon fled, for Mara, the spirit of the world and of sensual pleasure, the Buddhist devil, approached. For days Gautama withstood temptations of all kinds. . . .

At last the demon hosts gave up the struggle and Gautama, left alone, sank deeper and deeper into meditation. At the dawning of the forty-ninth day he knew the

Before his death (depicted here), Siddhartha Gautama urged his followers to continue to seek enlightenment, which might lead to nirvana.

truth. He had found the secret of sorrow, and understood at last why the world is full of suffering and unhappiness of all kinds, and what man must do to overcome them. He was fully enlightened—a Buddha. For another seven weeks he remained under the Tree of Wisdom (*bodhi*), meditating on the great truths he had found. . . . Leaving the Tree of Wisdom, he journeyed to the Deer Park near Varanasi (the modern Sarnath), where his five former disciples had settled to continue their penances.

To these five ascetics the Buddha preached his first sermon, or, in Buddhist phraseology, "set in motion the Wheel of the Law". The five were so impressed with his new doctrine that they gave up their austerities and once more became his disciples. A few days later a band of sixty young ascetics became his followers, and he sent them out in all directions to preach the Buddhist Dharma [doctrine]. Soon his name was well known throughout the Ganga Plain, and the greatest kings of the time favoured him and his followers. He gathered together a disciplined body of monks (called *bhiksus* . . . literally "beggers"), knit together by a common garb, the yellow robes of the order, and a common discipline, according to tradition laid down in detail by the Buddha himself. . . .

The First Buddhists

For eight months of the year the Buddha and his followers would travel from place to place, preaching to all and sundry. For the four months of the rainy season, roughly corresponding to the English summer, they would stop in one of the parks given to the Buddhist order by wealthy lay followers, living in huts of bamboo and reed—the first form of the great Buddhist monasteries of later times. For over forty years his reputation grew and the Sangha (literally Society, the Buddhist Order) increased in numbers and influence. . . . His ministry was a long, calm and peaceful one. . . .

The end came at the age of eighty. He spent the last rainy season of his life near the city of Vaisali, and after the rains he and his followers journeyed northwards to the hill country which had been the home of his youth. On the way he prepared his disciples for his death. He told them that his body was now like a worn-out cart, creaking at every joint. He declared that he had made no distinction between esoteric and exoteric teaching, but had preached the full doctrine to them. When he was gone they were to look for no new leader—the Doctrine (*Dharma*) which he had preached would lead them. They must rely on themselves, be their own lamps, and look for no refuge outside themselves.

The Buddha's First Teachings

attributed to Siddhartha Gautama

The original Buddha, Siddhartha Gautama, is said to have reached enlightenment outside the northern Indian town of Gaya. Afterward he wandered in the direction of Benares (Varanasi), a great city on the Ganges River, attracting a few disciples along the way. He preached his first sermon in Sarnath, on the outskirts of Benares. The following selection contains that first sermon, as well as two other early teachings. In them the Buddha informs his disciples of the "middle way" that will lead to the cessation of individual suffering and to the "great peace" of nirvana. The first sermon tells of the four noble truths, which each Buddhist must accept, and of the noble eightfold path, which each Buddhist tries to follow. The other teachings are reminders of the transitory nature of the body and of the world, attachment to which are obstacles on the path to enlightenment.

Although their origins cannot be completely confirmed, these teachings are thought by most Buddhists to have been memorized and recited first by Ananda, the Buddha's cousin and disciple, and thereafter by all devout monks. They were first written down in the first century B.C. in Sri Lanka in Pali, a language derived from Sanskrit, the ancient religious language of India.

John Walters, *The Essence of Buddhism*. New York: Thomas Y. Crowell, 1962.

The First Sermon

Brethren, there are two extremes which he who has given up the world should avoid.

What are these two extremes? One extreme is a life devoted to pleasures and lusts. For such a life is degrading, sensual, vulgar, profitless, and ignoble. And the other extreme is a life devoted to self-mortification. This is painful, ignoble, and profitless.

By avoiding these two extremes, the Tathagata [enlightened one; the Buddha himself] has obtained knowledge of the Middle Path, leading to calm, knowledge, insight, and [Nirvana].

What is the Middle Path that leads to these gifts? It is the Noble Eightfold Path consisting of right view, right resolution, right speech, right conduct, right livelihood, right effort, right mindfulness, right concentration.

This, brethren, is that Middle Path which brings knowledge, calm, insight, enlightenment, and [Nirvana].

Now, brethren, here is the Noble Truth about suffering:

Birth is suffering, illness is suffering, and death is suffering. To be near things we hate and to be separated from the things we like is suffering; and not to get what we want is suffering. Then this body, with its five aggregates [the body, feeling, conception, personality, and consciousness] of grasping, is suffering.

Now here is the Noble Truth about the arising of suffering:

It starts with the craving that leads to birth. It is accompanied by sensual pleasures demanding satisfaction, now here and now there. That is to say, craving to be reborn or craving for the end of rebirth.

Then this is the Noble Truth concerning the cessation of suffering:

It is the complete and passionless abandonment of this craving and the release from this craving.

Now the way leading to the cessation of suffering is that of the Noble Eightfold Path. That is to say, right view, right resolution, right speech, right conduct, right livelihood, right effort, right mindfulness, right concentration.

With my realization of the Noble Truths there came to me vision, insight, understanding, and illumination. And as I possessed in perfect purity this understanding of the Noble Truths, there came the realization that I had obtained supreme enlightenment in the world of men and gods.

Then knowledge and insight arose in me thus: "Sure is my release. This is my last birth. I shall not be born again."

Non-Self

"The body, brethren, is selfless, for it is destructible. Nor do sensation, perception, the predispositions, and consciousness together form the self. For if this were so, then consciousness would also not be destructible.

"What do you think?" the Buddha asked the five converts to whom he was preaching. "Is form permanent or transitory? And are sensation, perception, predispositions, and consciousness permanent or transitory?"

"They are transitory," replied the five.

"And is transitory evil or good?"

"Evil," they replied.

"Then can it be said of what is transitory, evil, and subject to change, 'This is "Mine," "I," "Myself"'?"

"No, this cannot be said," replied the five.

"Therefore, brethren, it must be admitted of every kind of physical form, past, present, or future, subjective or objective, distant or near, high or low, that 'This is not Mine, this is not I, this is not Myself.' And similarly it must be said of all sensations, perceptions, predispositions, and consciousness, 'These are not Mine, these are not I, these are not Myself.'

"And being aware of this, brethren, the true disciple will develop a disgust for physical form, for sensation, perception, predispositions, and consciousness. And so he will be stripped of desire. He becomes freed thereby and becomes aware of this freedom. And he knows that becoming has ended, that he has lived in purity, that he has done his duty and has forever ended mortality."

The Fire Sermon

All things, brethren, are burning. And what are all these things that are burning? The eye is on fire, forms are on fire, eye consciousness is on fire, the eye's impressions are on fire. And also on fire are all sensations originating from seeing—pleasant, unpleasant, or neutral.

And with what are all these burning? With fires of lust, hatred, and illusion; with birth, old age, death, mourning, misery, grief, and despair.

It is the same with the ear, the nose, tongue, and sense of touch. The mind also is on fire, thoughts are on fire. The conscious brain and impressions received by the brain, together with the sensations stirred by these, are also on fire.

With what are they burning? I say they are burning with the fires of lust, of hatred, and illusion. They are burning with the fires of birth, old age, sorrow, mourning, misery, grief, and despair.

Realizing this, brethren, the true disciple gets a disgust for the eye, for forms, for eye consciousness, for the eye's impressions, and the sensations thus arising. He also conceives disgust for the ear, nose, tongue, sense of touch, mind, thoughts, mind consciousness, impressions, and sensations.

Thus stripped of desire he is aware that he is freed. He knows there will be no more becoming, that he has lived in purity, that he has done his duty, and forever ended mortality.

Ashoka, Emperor of India, Spreads Buddhist Principles

by Stanley Wolpert

Buddhism remained a fairly small religion for two centuries after the life of the original Buddha, little more than one of the hundreds of variations of Hinduism that evolved in ancient India. It only became a major faith, and one clearly delineated from Hinduism, during and after the reign of the Indian emperor Ashoka, who reigned from 273 to 232 B.C. Ashoka himself may or may not have been a practicing Buddhist, as historian of India Stanley Wolpert notes in the following selection. But he strove to rule according to such fundamental Buddhist principles as nonviolence (ahimsa) and tolerance. The emperor also constructed pillars throughout his realm to remind his subjects of the importance of following moral teachings and remaining on the proper path, and he built thousands of stupas, or shrines, which served as centers for Buddhist rituals. Many of these pillars and stupas still stand.

Ashoka was the third king of the Mauryan dynasty, following Chandragupta and Bindusara. The Mauryans were the first kings to unite much of India into a single empire, and Ashoka completed the enterprise by defeating, in a violent war, the kingdom of Kalinga, the last major region to resist absorption into the Mauryan em-

pire. After the victory over Kalinga, Ashoka forsook violence and governed according to ahimsa and other religious teachings. His capital, Pataliputra, near modern
Patna in northern India, became a center of Buddhist
scholarship. Furthermore, India was a regional super-
power, and Ashoka used that power to help spread Buddhism to regions south and east, notably Sri Lanka and
Burma (Myanmar). Stanley Wolpert is a professor of Indian history at the University of California–Los Angeles.

For the first eight years of his reign, Ashoka behaved
as most ancient monarchs usually did, consolidating
and expanding his power in as ruthlessly expeditious a
manner as possible. Then, following the classical pre-
scription of the *Arthashastra* [an ancient Indian dis-
course on political power], which advised that "any
power superior in might to another should launch into
war," Ashoka invaded the frontier tribal kingdom of
Kalinga to his south (modern Orissa), subduing it after
the bloodiest war of his era. In the longest of his edicts,
Ashoka told of how many people were "slain," how
many more "died," and how many others were taken
"captive" from that conquered and settled land. With
its last major tribal opposition in South Asia annihi-
lated, the Mauryan [Ashoka's] administration could
now afford officially to abandon its policy of conquest
in favor of the more enlightened advocacy of peace and
nonviolence (*ahimsa*). Pillar edicts proclaimed Ashoka's
revulsion at past carnage and "remorse at having conquered Kalinga," which, it was said, made him resolve
thereafter to reject violence in favor of the Buddha's
law of nonviolence. Ashoka may actually have con-

verted to Buddhism in the tenth year of his reign, though whether or not he did is less important than the policy of pacification to which his newly unified empire was "converted." "If one hundredth part or one thousandth of those who died in Kalinga or were taken captive should now suffer similar fate," proclaimed the imperial edicts—which, though written in the name of a monarch whose epithets were "Beloved of the Gods" and "He of Gentle Visage," must be read as state propaganda issued by the bureaucratic machine—that "would be a matter of pain to His Majesty."

The Mauryan state [the empire of Ashoka], in the wake of the Kalinga conquest, thus proclaimed its emperor's resolve to bear "wrong" so far as "it can possibly be borne" without resorting to violent retribution, to "look kindly" upon all subjects, including the "forest tribes," though these were advised to "reform." Those who had not as yet surrendered to Mauryan rule, however, were warned to remember that the emperor was not only compassionate but powerful, using stick as well as carrot in completing the Mauryan settlement of South Asia, determined to ensure the "safety, self-control, peace of mind, and happiness" of all "animate beings" in the realm. Before the end of Ashoka's reign, Mauryan rule claimed revenue from Kashmir to Mysore, from Bangladesh to the heart of Afghanistan. Only three Dravidian "kingdoms" (Kerala, Chola, and Pandya) remained independent to its south, as did Ceylon. Mauryan India maintained diplomatic relations with all of its neighboring states, as well as with Antiochus II of Syria, Ptolemy II of Egypt, Antigonus Gonatas of Macedonia, and Alexander of Epirus. Ashoka was hailed as the first true *chakravartin* ("he for whom the wheel of the law turns"), universal emperor of India. He addressed all Indians as "my children" and carved in stone his paternalistic administration's express desire "that they may obtain every kind of welfare and happiness both in this world and the next." Ashoka was said to have informed his subordinates, doubtless to reassure them, that no matter where he was, whether eating or in his harem, he was always "on duty" to carry out the "business" of state. He may well have enjoyed the great power he wielded and pursued his imperial labors with religious dedication, but he could not administer so vast an empire alone. He appointed many special "overseers of the law" (*dhamma mahāmāttas*) to tour the empire as his emissaries to local governments, supervising local officials in the performance of their duties, which, given the great distances involved and the equally vast differences in customs, laws, and languages among India's diverse regions, must have been an almost impossible task. It was, nonetheless, the beginning of an attempt to enforce central bureaucratic control over what had hitherto been fiercely autonomous or virtually unsettled areas. We may safely assume that the regions most remote from Pāṭaliputra [Ashoka's capital city] were least profoundly affected by the periodic visits from central headquarters, but Ashoka's *mahāmāttas*, like later British collectors, showed the flag in the remotest corners of the realm, and that in itself was significant.

Living by and Advocating Buddhism

The surviving rock edicts of Ashoka are filled with good moral advice; they urge the Mauryans to "listen to father and mother," to practice "liberality to friends, relations, brahmans, and ascetics," and to abstain "from the slaughter of living creatures." Other key admonitions were toleration for all "sects," "compassion," and "truthfulness." *Dharma*, that unique word which means religion, law, duty, and responsibility, was used more than any other term by Ashoka, who deemed it "most excellent." In his twenty-sixth year, the emperor inscribed the following message: "Both this world and the other are hard to reach, except by great love of the law, great self-examination, great obedience, great respect, great energy . . . this is my rule: government by the law, administration according to the law, gratification of my subjects under the law, and protection through the law." Ashoka abandoned the traditional annual royal hunt in favor of a "pilgrimage of religious law," which allowed him to visit distant corners of his empire personally, the living symbol of imperial unity to his people, who must have viewed him as a divinity incarnate. To facilitate communication throughout the empire and accelerate the process of integration, Ashoka had shade trees planted along the roads over which he journeyed, and sponsored from his treasury such public works as the digging of wells and the erection of rest houses on major highways built in his reign. Thanks to Ashoka's conversion to *ahimsa*, many more Indians became vegetarians at this time. The emperor's personal example was used, moreover, to help inspire millions beyond his domain, for his emissaries were sent to convert the peoples of Ceylon and Burma, and possibly of more distant regions of Southeast Asia, to Buddhism, and through Buddhism to Mauryan pacification and Indian civilization.

Sometime between 250 and 240 B.C. Ashoka hosted the Third Great Council of Buddhism at Pātaliputra, which had by then become Asia's foremost center of art and culture. The Ashokan pillars were topped by capitals decorated with animal sculpture, the most famous of which are the four lions of Samath, three of whom have become the national symbol of modern India. The lions supported an enormous stone "wheel of the law," commemorating the Buddha's first sermon at Samath, and they rose above an abacus around which were carved four smaller wheels and four animals—an elephant, a horse, a lion, and a bull. . . .

The King as Temple Builder

Tradition credits Ashoka with having built no fewer than 84,000 *stupas* (literally "gathered"), or Buddhist reliquary mounds, among which the ashes of the Buddha were supposedly subdivided from the eight original *stupas* erected earlier. These hemispherical mounds of solid stone, the largest and most famous of which was erected at Sanchi in central India, were subsequently worshipped by Buddhists, who would circumambulate the *stupa* in a clockwise direction. Centuries after Ashoka's death the *stupas* were embellished with elaborately designed stone railings and gates topped with many tiers of umbrellas above the "little square house" (*hārmika*), set over the egg-shaped mound, through which the Buddha's spirit was said to pass from terrestrial to celestial release and eternal repose. The multitiered umbrellas are seen by some art historians as the architectural prototype of the East Asian pagoda, later introduced into China by those indefatigable cultural couriers of early Asian history, the Buddhist missionary monks. *Stupas* were further evidence of the vigorous revival of Indian interest in and patronage for monumental art, and they may in fact be a stone version of the earlier, less permanent Aryan sacrificial mounds. The *stupa* seems, at any rate, to have symbolized the universe, and it may, therefore, be viewed as a primitive ancestor of the Hindu temple, which was later to share with it such microcosmic meaning. . . .

Ashoka seems to have withdrawn almost entirely from public life during the last years of his reign, which ended with his death in 232 B.C. Following Ashoka, Mauryan rule lost much of its vitality, falling into economic as well as spiritual decline. The coins were soon debased and the ramparts of empire attacked and eroded in north and south alike. Many sons contested the throne, and there is no consensus among Indian sources as to whom it went, though Kunala, his son Samprati, and Ashoka's grandson Dasharatha are highest on the list of immediate successors. The technological obstacles to integration and the cost of so enormous a bureaucracy soon made a fiction of centralized Mauryan imperial rule, however. With power so attenuated by the attempt to maintain that rule, it is hardly surprising to find that fragmentation, local reassertion of independence, and interregional rivalries and invasions swiftly followed the demise of the God-King-Father Ashoka. Nonetheless, the first great dynasty of Indian history continued to rule over Magadha at least until 184 B.C., when Brihadratha, last of the Mauryans, was killed by his brahman [high-caste Hindu] general, Pushyamitra Shunga, who started a new line of rajas in central India that ruled a much diminished "empire" until 72 B.C. India's first great unification thus lasted 140 years; it was won by the swords of Chandragupta and Bindusara, ruled in accord with the shrewd pragmatism of the *Arthashastra*, and consolidated under the royal paternalism of Ashoka, whose toleration for peoples of every faith, tongue, and stage of development accepted the realities of the Indian subcontinent's regional pluralism and extended over all a single system's "white umbrella" of righteous law. Less surprising than its disintegration in the wake of northern invasions, southern defections, and constant bickerings over succession is the fact that the idea of unity survived so long at so early a state of technological integration of the subcontinent—for, after all, the Mauryans ruled India roughly as long as the British would more than two thousand years later.

Two Teachings on Right and Wrong Behavior

attributed to Siddhartha Gautama

The following selection is from the Dharmapada, one of the canonical Buddhist texts that are believed to have been derived from sermons and teachings of the original Buddha. They were first memorized and recited by monks and then written down, in the Indian languages of Pali or Sanskrit, in the first century B.C. Buddhist scholars and devotees consider the Dharmapada an authoritative work representing the Buddha's teachings.

The two teachings in this selection are concerned with morality and behavior, using the word *karma* to denote the spiritual consequences of behavior. The second, in particular, emphasizes what the Buddha called the "middle path," which leads to worldly happiness.

The Chapter on Karma

1. A single rule you set aside, or lying words you speak,
The world beyond you ridicule—no evil you won't do!

2. Better for you to swallow a ball of iron red-hot and flaming with fire,

Than on the alms of the people to live, while immoral, indulgent, intemperate.

Siddhartha Gautama, "Verses from the Sanskrit Dharmapada," *The Dhammapada*, edited by Anne Bancroft. Rockport, MA: Element Books, 1997.

3. If it's suffering you fear, if it's suffering you dislike,
Just do no evil deeds at all—for all to see or secretly.

4. Even a flight in the air cannot free you from suffering, After the deed which is evil has once been committed.

5. Not in the sky nor in the ocean's middle,
Nor if you were to hide in cracks in mountains,
Can there be found on this wide earth a corner
Where karma does not catch up with the culprit.

6. But if you see the evil others do, and if you feel you disapprove,
Be careful not to do likewise, for people's deeds remain with them.

7. Those who cheat in business deals, those who act against the Dharma! [Buddhist Law],
Those who swindle, those who trick—not only harm their fellow-men,
They hurl themselves into a gorge, for people's deeds remain with them.

8. Whatever deeds a man may do, be they delightful, be they bad,
They make a heritage for him; deeds do not vanish without trace.

9. A man will steal while profit seems to lie that way.
Then others steal from him, and so the thief by thieving is undone.

10. The fool, while sinning, thinks and hopes, 'This never will catch up with me'.
Wait till you're in the other world, and there the fate of sinners learn!

11. The fool, while sinning, thinks and hopes, 'This never will catch up with me'.
But later on there's bitterness, when punishment must be endured.

12. The fool does evil deeds while unaware of what they lead to.

By his own deeds the stupid man is burnt, as though burnt up by fire.

13. The fools, unwise, behave as though they were their own worst enemies,

Committing many evil deeds which issue then in bitter fruits.

14. Not is an action called 'well done', which makes us suffer afterwards,

Of which we reap the fruit in tears, with weeping, wailing and lament.

15. That action only is 'well done', which brings no suffering in its train,

Of which we reap the fruit quite glad, in happiness, with joyous heart.

16. In hot pursuit of their own joys they laugh when they do evil deeds.

They'll weep with pain and misery, when they receive their punishment.

17. An evil deed need not at once cause trouble to the man who did it.

It keeps up with the careless fool, just as a fire, smouldering under ashes.

18. Just like a new-forged blade the evil deed need not at once cause any wounds.

Wait till you're in the other world, and there the fate of sinners learn!

For later on there's bitterness, when punishment must be endured.

19. The iron itself createth the rust,

Which slowly is bound to consume it.

The evil-doer by his own deeds

Is led to a life full of suffering.

The Chapter on Morality

1. If you want honour, wealth, or, after death, a blissful life among the gods,
Then take good care that you observe the precepts of a moral life!
2. 3. The prudent man will lead a moral life
When he considers it has four rewards:
A sense of virtue gives him peace,
His body is not over-taxed,
At night he sleeps a happy sleep,
And when he wakes, he wakes with joy.
A holy man, endowed with vision,
He thrives and prospers in this world.
4. How excellent a moral life pursued till death!
How excellent a well-established faith!
And wisdom is for men a treasure which brings merit,
And which the thieves find very hard to steal.
5. The man of wisdom who did good,
The man of morals who gave gifts,
In this world and the next one too,
They will advance to happiness.
6. 7. His moral habits planted firm, his senses well protected,
In eating temperate, and to vigilance inclined,
The monk who feels no weariness, and struggles day and night,
His progress is assured, and he shall win Nirvana soon.
8. 9. His moral habits planted firm, his trance and wisdom first-rate,
Unwearied, zealous, he shall gain, the end of ill for ever.

Let him thus always moral be, preserve his meditation,

And train his insight constantly, a man of thoughtful habits!

10. The wise, his fetters burst, the urge for further life exhausted,

No more the prospect of rebirth for him at death, but full release.

11. The man whose moral habits, trances, wise reflections are full-grown,

Secure for ever, pure and happy, he is then exempt from ever coming back again.

12. Free from his fetters, unattached, with perfect knowledge, without will to live,

Raised high above the range of Mara's [the god of death's] realms, he blazes radiant as the sun.

13. When a monk is full of himself, is heedless and given to things that are outside,

He can never make progress in moral perfection, in trance or in wisdom.

14. Rain presses down on what is covered, but what is open lets it through;

Uncover therefore what is covered, and so the rain will do no harm.

15. The wise will always carefully observe the moral rules,

Thus clearing rapidly the path that to Nirvana leads them.

16. The scent of flowers travels with the wind,

The scent of jasmine travels not against it.

The odour of the good pervades in all directions,

Their fragrance spreads, whatever be the wind.

17. Sandalwood or tagara scent, lotus flower or jasmine spray,

Nobler than the perfume of all is the fragrance of virtuous lives.

18. Sandalwood or tagara shrubs, trifling the scent which they emit,

Virtuous lives send their fragrance up high to the gods that are above.

19. If your morality is pure, if you are always wakeful and attentive,

If you are freed by knowledge of the truth, then Mara cannot find you when you die.

20. This is the path which to safety leads,

This is the path which brings purity.

If you but tread it, and meditate,

Then you'll escape from Mara's bonds!

The Spread of Buddhism

by Christmas Humphreys

Although Buddhism was born in India and had its origins in Hinduism, it remains a minor religion there. Only during the reign of Ashoka in the third century B.C. could Buddhism be said to be a dominant faith in India. Instead, Buddhism grew to be the most important religion in most of the nations of east Asia and Southeast Asia. In the following selection, writer and British Buddhist Christmas Humphreys describes the many ways in which Buddhism spread to those regions in the centuries after Ashoka's rule. Throughout, Humphreys notes the political as well as religious contexts in which Buddhism took hold, while also emphasizing that Buddhism was often integrated with earlier practices and beliefs. He delineates three broad forms of Buddhism. The first, which took hold in Sri Lanka (Ceylon), Burma, and Thailand, was Theravada Buddhism. Also known as the "smaller path," Theravada was the last surviving sect of the traditional, conservative Buddhism practiced by many of the Buddha's first followers. The second form, Mahayana Buddhism, or the "greater path," took hold in east Asia, and it tended to be looser and less doctrinaire than Theravada. The third form, found in such countries as Cambodia, Laos, and Vietnam, represented various combinations of Buddhist practices, Chinese and Hindu influences, and even earlier religions.

Christmas Humphreys is the author of a number of books on Buddhism, including *Exploring Buddhism* and *The Twelve Principles of Buddhism.*

Buddhism was from the first a missionary religion. Within a few days of the First Sermon the Buddha sent his handful of converts into the world with the famous [monks] exhortation 'Go ye forth, O Bhikkhus, for the gain of the many, for the welfare of the many, in compassion for the world. Proclaim the Doctrine glorious, preach ye a life of holiness, perfect and pure.' And the same command appears in the Mahayana work *The Voice of the Silence.* 'Point out the Way—however dimly, and lost among the host—as does the evening star to those who tread their path in darkness. Give light and comfort to the toiling pilgrim, and seek out him who knows still less than thou, who in his wretched desolation sits starving for bread of Wisdom—let him hear the Law.' For part of Buddha's task was to make available to all men the universal principles of truth which the Brahmans [teachers of Hinduism] of his day considered their monopoly, and Buddhism was from the first a Message for all mankind.

To proclaim a Teaching, however, is not to proselytize in the sense of forcing ideas upon an unwilling audience, much less to use pressure to obtain adherence to one's own point of view. A man's sole right, a right which to the Buddhist is also a duty, is to offer to all the knowledge of a path which the Buddha proclaimed as a way to Enlightenment, and which the speaker or writer, so far as he has trodden that Path, has found to be true. Some seed, of course, will fall on stony around, but some will flourish abundantly, and 'the gift of the Dhamma [or Dharma, the Buddhist path] is greater than all other gifts'.

Nor did the Buddha preach 'Buddhism' to his monks, although they in the course of centuries gradually codified in formulas what once was given as a living stream of spiritual experience. The Tathagata [enlightened one] pointed out the nature of the manifested universe and the Path which leads from the world of appearances to ultimate Reality. He dealt with life, not with the changing forms of it, and life can never be locked away in glorious phrases. The Buddha's Teaching was a mode of living, a method of approach to life itself. Buddhism is man's attempt to create a cage for this experience, and to the extent that he succeeds he fails to inherit the Wisdom which the Master offered to mankind. . . .

Buddhism in Sri Lanka

The earliest definite mission was to Ceylon [known today as Sri Lanka]. Asoka, who sent his ambassadors to most of the known world, sent, at the invitation of King Tissa, the Thera Mahendra (Pali: Mahinda), who was either the son or the younger brother of the Emperor. The mission was apparently a great success. According to the *Dipavamsa* (fourth [century]) and the *Mahavamsa* (fifth [century]), two famous Sinhalese [Sri Lanka's language] records, the founding of Buddhism in Ceylon was attended with most notable miracles, but, however this may be, several of the Chinese pilgrims who visited the island centuries later confirmed that the inhabitants of Lanka, the name for Ceylon which figures largely in Indian history, accepted the new faith with avidity, and in spite of Tamil invasions from South India and later European aggression, it remains the proud stronghold of the Theravada to this day. . . .

In the third century A.D. Ceylon was still further honoured with a tooth of the Buddha, which has become a national treasure. Insurance reverence is paid to this relic at the Temple of the Tooth at Kandy, and even if some historians claim that the original was burnt by the Catholic Portuguese, the Sinhalese reply that what was burnt was only a substitute.

Meanwhile the Sangha [order of Buddhist monks and nuns] was engaged in more valuable enterprises than relic worship, for it is recorded that in the first century B.C. the memorized [Pali] Canon [authorized texts] was reduced to writing, a historic fact which excuses to some extent the excessive honour paid by the Sinhalese to-day to the written word. The fifth century produced the first Buddhist commentator in Buddhaghosa, a Brahman convert to Buddhism from Gaya, His *Visuddhi-magga* ('Path of Purity'), written in Pali, maintains the original Arhat [enlightened] ideal, and crystallizes, as it were, the Theravada view of the original Message of the Buddha.

In the eleventh century Ceylon was being hard pressed by the Cholas of South India, and it seems that the Dhamma, too, had fallen on hard times, for the king of Ceylon sent to the king of Burma for Bhikkhus to strengthen the native Sangha. A century later, however, there was a great revival of Buddhism under King Parakrama Bahu, and according to [scholar of Buddhist art] Dr [Reginald] Le May, 'from that time up to the sixteenth century Ceylon was regarded by its brother Buddhist countries, Siam, Burma and Cambodia, with almost as much veneration as the holy places of Buddhism in India, as the fountain-head of the pure Theravada doctrines'.

Buddhism in Burma

The earliest history of Buddhism in Burma [today also known as Myanmar] is obscure. Asoka sent his missionaries to 'Suvannabhumi' (The Golden Land), which apparently means Burma, and the Indian infiltration of influence by land and sea must have brought with it the prevailing forms of Indian Buddhism. Some Burmese claim Buddhaghosa as the source of their Buddhism, but the early chronicles of Ceylon make no such claim. The great man's influence, however, was enormous, and may well have affected the mixture of Mahayana and Hinayana [another word for Theravada] Buddhism and indigenous *nat* (a kind of nature-spirit) worship which satisfied Burma for the first 1,000 years A.D. Even to-day the Sanskrit terms in Burmese Buddhism are evidence of its Mahayana origin, and as [religious scholar] Kenneth Saunders says, 'Burmese Buddhists have a vague, pantheistic philosophy of life which is more akin to the Mahayana than the Hinayana', and for reasons given he concludes that 'the Buddhism of the Burmese masses is somewhere between the Hinayana and the Mahayana'.

The worship of *nats*, akin to the worship of *devatas* in Ceylon, is incurable, as [religious scholar] J.B. Pratt says, 'The Burman loves the Buddha but fears the nats. The Buddha he knows will never harm him, but the nats may!' But it is well said that if you scratch a Burman you will find a Buddhist [underneath]. Behind the façade of a gay and a frivolous people is an intense love of the Buddha, and no force, political or otherwise, will ever remove it from their lives.

The greatest figure in Burmese Buddhism is King Anawrahta of Pagan (A.D. 1044–1077), who, being converted to Theravada Buddhism by a Shin Arahan, a wandering Bhikkhu from the neighbouring kingdom of Thaton, sent for full instruction, and Burma officially became thereafter attached to the Theravada School. The king soon made his capital city one of the wonders of the world, and such temple building has seldom been seen, Hundreds of Gothic churches were then rising all over Europe, but thousands of pagodas rose in a few square miles in Pagan, while one of the greatest temples on earth was raised about a century later in Rangoon, to dominate the city, then as now, with its pinnacle of plated gold. Here, too, in the Shwe Dagon [Pagoda in Rangoon], are enshrined relics of the Buddha, and this curious blend of market and forum with a holy place of pilgrimage is undoubtedly one of the world centres of Buddhism.

In the thirteenth century [Mongol emperor] Kublai Khan attacked Pagan and sacked it, and not till the sixteenth century was Burma again united as a Buddhist kingdom. Then came the British who, as elsewhere, respected the Triple Gem of the Buddha, Dhamma and Sangha, and to-day the orange robe of the Order, like the yellow robe of Siam and Ceylon, still dominates the landscape. The Siamese claim that their Sangha leads in the Vinaya Pitaka, the Rules of the Order; the Sinhalese Sangha, which at present produces the leading minds of Theravada Buddhism, concentrates on the Sutta Pitaka, the teachings of the Buddha. The Burmese Sangha, as the visitor will be told a dozen times before he is a week in the country, is master of the Abhidhamma, that complex mixture of metaphysics, psychology and mind-development which partly derives from Indian Yoga. This deliberate choice is further evidence that Burma began its Buddhist life as part of the Mahayana, although it is to-day, and has been for the last 1,000 years, a stronghold, like Ceylon and Siam, of the Theravada School.

Buddhism in Thailand

It is probable that the people now known as the Siamese (or Thai) contacted Buddhism before migrating South from their native China. To-day, the interrelation of the various races and cultures which fill this south-east corner of Asia is so complex that it is difficult to isolate any single factor. The Burmese, meaning a compound of Burmese, Karens, Shans, Talaings, and Arakanese, and the Cambodians (Khmers), Chams, Annamese, Laos and others, who have fought each other, ruled each other and affected each other in the last 2,000 years, acquired at some time first, apparently, Mahayana Buddhism and later the Theravada, but when and whence and how it is hard to say.

By A.D. 1200 the Siamese were settled in their present territory, and indeed in a much wider area until deprived of a large part of it by acquisitive Western 'Powers'. In the fourteenth century, the King of the day, inspired by whom we know not, sent to Ceylon for a Theravadin Bhikkhu, who was received with considerable honour at the then capital, Sukhotai, and was created Sangharaja, or Supreme Head of the Order. The King, following Asoka's example, entered the Order, and from this springs the close connexion between the royal house and the Sangha which is a noticeable feature of Siamese Buddhism to-day.

Thus the trinity of the Theravada, Ceylon, Burma and Siam, with all that matters in common, proudly maintains its joint tradition of preserving at least reasonably intact the essential Teaching of the All-Enlightened One.

Buddhism in Cambodia

South-east Asia is vaguely claimed by the Theravada, but much of it is so heavily influenced by China, and an earlier Hinduism, that it is difficult to substantiate such a claim for more than Cambodia. Until the fourteenth century the religion of Cambodia was a blend of Hinduism and Mahayana Buddhism; hence the complex history and art of the famous temple of Angkor. Later, the Siamese influence became paramount, and with it a Theravada ascendancy.

Buddhism in China

There is a strong tradition that Buddhism reached China early in the Han Dynasty (first century B.C.), but there is historic evidence that in A.D. 61 the Emperor Ming-ti, in consequence of a dream, sent messengers to India for Buddhist books and teachers. Two monks returned to the Emperor's capital of Lo-yang laden with images and scriptures of the Mahayana School. One of their Indian companions translated the *Sutra of 42 Sections* into Chinese, and thus began the tremendous task of making known the splendour of Indian Buddhism to the Confucian and Taoist scholars of the day. This Sutra is an anthology of precepts, largely Theravada in spirit, but its influence was soon swamped by later translations, and although the Pali Scriptures are studied to this day in

China and Japan it was the Mahayana School whose doctrines the Chinese were asked to accept, and which they accepted only after a modification so profound as all but to create a new form of Buddhism.

The new arrivals were not received with open arms. Their doctrines were too subtle and metaphysical for the essentially practical, not to say material, Chinese mind, and the disciples of Confucius objected to the habit of monkhood, then unknown in China. It meant that men avoided their primary task of parenthood, whereby they continued the line of filial respect, and, what was nearly as objectionable, it taught them to beg instead of working for their living. Moreover, whereas in Ceylon and Burma and Siam the Indian culture entered a land inferior in development, the Chinese culture of the late Han Dynasty was second to none. Confusian and Taoist ideals, almost exactly complementary, filled the minds of the cultured levels of society and both, being indigenous, combined to cold-shoulder the alien ideas from the West. It is not surprising therefore, that it was only after three hundred years of effort that Buddhism joined the other two philosophies to form the famous tripod of the Chinese religion.

Success was largely due to the work of the translator Kumarajiva (fourth and fifth centuries A.D.). His output was so enormous that a new wave of interest was created, which culminated in permission to the Buddhist laymen to become monks and to found a Chinese branch of the Sangha. Thereafter Chinese Buddhism, though continuing to receive support from India, was native and largely independent, and by the sixth century most of North-West China was Buddhist, though largely, it would seem, of the Pure Land, or Amida, School.

Up to this time, however, Indian Buddhism was still

but an alien study, albeit a popular study, for the intelligentsia. It had not yet been translated into a native idiom. This was the work of Bodhidharma (Chinese: Tamo; Japanese: Daruma), an Indian Buddhist from Conjeeveram, near Madras, whose brilliant, ruthless mind made short work of the prevailing speculative thought and its companion, salvation by faith. Apparently without the least intention of doing so he founded the School which, within a few hundred years, was almost commensurate with Chinese Buddhism.

The purpose and technique of the School were early summarized:

> A special transmission outside the scriptures;
> No dependence upon words and letters;
> Direct pointing to the soul of man;
> Seeing into one's own nature.

In this famous summary Bodhidharma claimed to be returning to the spirit of the Buddha's teaching. This, he claimed, was *Dhyana* [meditation]: hence his School was called, from the Chinese corruption of Dhyana, Ch'an, corrupted in turn by the Japanese into Zen. As such it passed in the twelfth century into Japan, and after fifteen hundred years is still one of the two main influences in the spiritual life of that country. It still represents such life as remains in Chinese Buddhism.

Buddhism reached its greatest strength in China in the T'ang Dynasty (620–907), when it combined with the Chinese native genius to produce some of the greatest art—some think the greatest art—which the world has known. Moreover, the steady stream of Buddhist scholars who came to China from India brought with them the science and medicine of the day, while it was the monks in China who originated printing by blocks, the first work to be so printed being the *Dia-*

mond Sutra, still one of the most popular scriptures in China or Japan.

In China Buddhism suffered its first persecution, and for centuries its elevation or suppression turned upon whether the Emperor of the day was a Confucian or Buddhist devotee. But the double process of importation and assimilation went on steadily. The Chinese pilgrim monks, Fa-Hien, Hiuen-Tsiang, I-Tsing and others, from whom we learn so much of Buddhist history in India, continued to arrive with Sutras for translation, and strange and disturbing ideas. Of the various Schools of Buddhism, the Ch'an (Zen) School was, by the end of the Ming Dynasty (1368–1644), paramount. Yet even the virile Zen which, under the tremendous impetus of Hui-neng (Wei Lang), the sixth (Chinese) Patriarch, had filled the countryside with monasteries and centres of learning, began to fail under the rule of the Manchus. It is true that the greatest of the Manchu Emperors, K'ang-Hsi (1662–1723) and C'hien Lung (1736–1795), never suppressed the Buddhist religion, and even showed it favour, but under their rule Confucianism achieved its final ascendancy. The decline of Buddhism in China, however, was not produced by the failure of royal patronage, and was caused, as decline is usually caused, by its own debility.

Buddhism in Korea

As [religious scholar] Sir Charles Eliot says, 'The Buddhism of Korea cannot be sharply distinguished from the Buddhism of China and Japan . . . there is little originality in art: in literature and doctrine none at all. Buddhism, together with Chinese writing, reached Korea about A.D. 372, but though it flourished exceedingly for several centuries it was never entirely acclimatized, and when in the thirteenth century a wave of Confucian reaction arrived from China the Korean Court accepted its influence with avidity, and the Buddhist leaders of the day were unable to cope with the 'new' and popular teaching. Thereafter Buddhist influence began to decline, and what remains of it to-day is almost entirely the dynamic Zen.

The importance of Korea in the history of Buddhism is as a conduit pipe between China and Japan, and it is therefore important to note that type of Buddhism which was available to cross the narrow seas. Kenneth Saunders, who spent some time in its beautifully sited mountain monasteries, says it is 'clearly a mixed Buddhism of the "accommodated" Mahayana, with Sakya Muni [the Buddha] as a central figure, with meditation as the chief exercise, with the philosophy of the Void and the T'ien t'ai (Jap.: Tendai) classification tacitly assumed, and yet with some pietistic tendencies, as is evidenced by the place given to the Buddha of the Western Paradise'. Even to-day the fierce technique of Chinese Zen is maintained, and R.H. Blyth, author of *Zen in English Literature*, who spent sixteen years in Korean monasteries, has described to the author the uncompromising severity of life and spiritual discipline which he found maintained. If, therefore, Korean Buddhism is failing in quantity, its quality survives.

Buddhism in Japan

Buddhism entered Japan from Korea in A.D. 552. There was mild resistance from certain quarters, but in the famous Regent Shotoku Taishi (593–622) the Buddhists found as their patron and leader one of the greatest men whom Japan has produced. A contemporary of Muhammad [the founder of Islam] and St Augustine of Canterbury [a Christian thinker], Prince Shotoku's own influence was no less profound than theirs in his own country. He largely built the city of Nara, and in Horyuji, completed in A.D. 607, he built a monastic settlement which became the prototype of Japanese architecture to this day. Native craftsmen, taught by artist-craftsmen of all kinds imported from China and Korea, not only built the great shrines and temples, many of which survive today, but wrought great images of bronze and wood, painted the frescoes of Horyuji which ranked, until destroyed by fire in 1949, with the best of Ajanta [a noted Indian monastery], and founded standards of culture which the Japanese, always brilliant in adaptation, had within a few years made their own. Nor was the Prince content with patronage. He wrote himself a series of commentaries on the *Saddharma Pundarika*, the *Vimalakirti Sutra* and the *Srimala Sutra* [all early Buddhist texts from India], and by this selection went far to formulate Japanese Buddhism.

But the Buddhism which entered Japan under his patronage was already divided into rival schools, and although they developed peacefully side by side in the thousand years which followed, and were added to by indigenous sects, there was no attempt at co-ordination, and it was not until the time of the famous fourteen 'Fundamental Buddhistic Beliefs', as formulated by Colonel [Henry Steel] Olcott [an early Western Buddhist] in 1891, and the present writer's 'Twelve Principles of Buddhism', approved by all Japanese Schools in 1946, that a common ground was found for Buddhism as distinct from the varying forms of it to be found in the different schools. . . .

In China Buddhism was always a religion without political affinities; in Japan it was early an 'established' cult under Court favour. Zen at least was a major factor in the development of Bushido, the equivalent of our medieval knighthood, and as such an active participant in the complex internecine struggles of the 'closed' period of Japanese history. For most of its life a protégé of the Shoguns [political leaders], Japanese Buddhism therefore suffered a serious loss of revenue and prestige with the abolition of the Shogunate in 1868. With the usual adaptability of the Japanese character, however, it weathered the storm, and reorganized itself as a disestablished Church. Now that Shinto [an indigenous Japanese religion], too, has been 'disestablished', the field is clear for any and every religion to attract the Japanese mind, and if the Shin and Zen Schools of Buddhism between them rule the minds of the vast majority of Japanese, it is mainly because between them they satisfy all complementary needs of the human mind. Yet it is certainly true to say that to the extent that Ceylon, Siam and Burma are Buddhist countries of the Theravada School, Japan is a Buddhist country of the Mahayana, and as the Buddhism of China is rapidly dying, and that of Tibet is in a sense a School of its own, Japan is now the country in which the Mahayana in all its aspects can best be considered and described.

CHAPTER 2

The Smaller Path:
Theravada Buddhism
in Southeast Asia

Religions and Religious Movements

Buddhism and Kingship in Sri Lanka

by Trevor Ling

One of the first places outside of India to which Buddhism spread is the large island off India's southeastern coast known today as Sri Lanka. Sri Lanka had long been within India's orbit before Buddhism's arrival: The Hindu epic poem the Ramayana is partially set in "Lanka," and even today Theravada Buddhists cherish their modified versions of the poem. The people of Sri Lanka, the Sinhalese, always maintained a sense of ethnic and cultural separation from their large neighbor, however, and even after Buddhism faded in India it remained strong in Sri Lanka. The island nation came to be considered the stronghold of the Theravada path, that form of Buddhism following most closely the original teachings of the Buddha and his disciples. Indeed, many of the basic texts of Buddhism were first written down in Sri Lanka in the first century B.C. in Pali, an Indian language.

In the following selection, religious scholar Trevor Ling examines the relationship between kingship and Buddhist practices, focusing mainly on the period from 1153 to 1186, the reign of a devout and model-setting king known as Parakkama Bahu I, a major figure in a Sinhalese historical chronicle known as the *Culavamsa.*

Trevor Ling, *The Buddha: Buddhist Civilization in India and Ceylon.* London: Temple Smith, 1973. Copyright © 1973 by Trevor Ling. Reproduced by permission of Ashgate Publishing, Ltd.

Ling notes that despite the passage of many centuries, the king followed many of the principles of a predecessor, the Buddhist Indian king Ashoka, who reigned during the third century B.C., and who was thought to have sent the first Buddhist disciples to Sri Lanka. During the decades when it was part of the British Empire, the common name for the island was Ceylon, the term Ling uses. But in recent years "Sri Lanka" has been reestablished as the country's official name. Trevor Ling is the author of many books on Buddhism, including *Buddhism and the Mythology of Evil*, *Buddhist Revival in India*, and *Buddhist Imperialism and War*.

Of the *Culavamsa* [a historical chronicle covering the years 362–1813] as a whole, approximately a third is devoted to one king, Parakkama Bahu I, whose reign covered the period 1153–1186 A.D. Just as in the first and second parts of the *Mahavamsa* [a chronicle covering earlier eras] it is Devanam-piya Tissa and Duttha-gamini who stand out as the central figures, to be given epic treatment, in the continuation, the *Culavamsa*, it is undoubtedly Parakkama Bahu who receives this treatment 'There is no name in the annals of Sinhalese history', writes Dr. [G.P.] Malalasekere, 'which commands the veneration of the people in such measure as that of this prince of the "mighty arm", Parakkama Bahu, since he united in his person the piety of Devanam-piya Tissa and the chivalry of Duttha-gamini.'

A good deal of change had occurred in the Buddhist state of Ceylon, however, between their reigns and his. There had been changes in the nature of Buddhism, both within the *Sangha* [Buddhist community] itself, and in the popular practices which had come to be associated with Buddhism among the people as a whole, and there had been considerable social change, mostly in the direction of a decline in the general welfare, both of the nobility and of the poorer people. At the outset of his reign as king of Ceylon, from his new capital at Polonnaruva, Parakkama Bahu, we are told, thought thus: 'By those kings of old who turned aside from the trouble of furthering the laity and the Order . . . has this people aforetime been grievously harassed. May it henceforth be happy and may the Order of the great Sage—long sullied by admixture with a hundred false doctrines, rent assunder by the schism of the three fraternities and flooded with numerous unscrupulous *bhikkus* [monks] whose sole task is the filling of their bellies—that Order which though five thousand years have not yet passed is in a state of decay, once more attain stability. Of those people of noble birth who here and there have been ruined, I would fain by placing them again in their rightful position, become the protector in accordance with tradition. Those in search of help I would fain support by letting like a cloud overspreading the four quarters of the earth a rich rain of gifts pour continually down upon them.' His intention is seen to be three-fold: first, to reform and purify the Order, which had been affected by what today would be called revisionist doctrines, and purge its ranks of imposters and idlers; second, to restore to their proper status the dignitaries of the land; and third, to make provision for the sick and the needy. The chronicle then describes how all this was carried out, and is confirmed by epigraphical evidence.

After describing the achievements of this great reign in detail for some six chapters, or 987 verses, the chronicler brings his account of the reign to a close with the words, 'Thus Parakkama Bahu, the Ruler of men, by whom were performed divers and numerous kinds of meritorious works, who continually found the highest satisfaction in the teaching of the Master [the Buddha], who was endowed with extraordinary energy and discernment, carried on the government for thirty-three years.'

Royal Support for Shrines and Health Centers

A great deal of attention is devoted by the chronicler to describing Parakkama Bahu's policy and practice because it was an outstanding example of the Buddhist ideal, although by no means the only example. Other kings of Ceylon, before and after him, approximated to this same ideal. Generous provision for the *Sangha*, and support for them in the study, preservation and public teaching of the Buddhist tradition was a primary duty of the kings of Ceylon. The building and equipping of shrines, in order to encourage the practices of meditation and the honouring of the Buddha was another equally characteristic feature. Vigorous measures for improving the material condition of the people were also an important part of the Buddhist ruler's proper exercise of his power. The ensuring of an adequate food supply for a growing population required large irrigation works, and these were frequently undertaken by the Sinhalese kings. Dhatusena, for example, is remembered for the large reservoir which he had built, covering an area of ten square miles, whose waters were conveyed to the dry areas where they were needed by a canal fifty-four miles long. Parakkama Bahu was the author of a scheme to provide island-wide irrigation. 'In the realm that is subject to me', he said, 'there are, apart

from many strips of country where the harvest flour-
ishes mainly by rain water, but few fields which are dependent on rivers with permanent flow, or on great

*A statue of the Buddha sits in Polonnaruwa, Sri Lanka. Sri Lanka is
one of the first places outside of India to which Buddhism spread.*

reservoirs. Also, by many mountains, by thick jungle, and by widespread swamps my kingdom is much straitened. Truly in such a country not even a little water that comes from the rain must flow into the ocean without being made useful to man.' According to the chronicles he made good the damage which time and neglect had done to the irrigation works constructed by earlier kings, and in addition carried out new construction projects which far exceeded the scope of anything which had been done previously.

Another characteristic feature of Sinhalese Buddhist civilization was the attention which was given to establishing and maintaining centres for the treatment of the sick. 'This was the most highly advanced branch of the social services provided for the people by the state', observes [historian of Sri Lanka] C.W. Nicholas. 'The Chronicles often record additional endowments to the national medical service by several kings, and these statements are fully corroborated by the inscriptions. High dignitaries of state also founded or endowed hospitals. There were, in addition to general hospitals, homes for cripples, the blind and the incurable. Lying-in [birthing] homes for women were established in several localities. Sick animals were also cared for.'

It is important to recognize the extent to which all this was associated with adherence to Buddhist values. The kings who were most active in promoting the welfare of their people were also most prominently concerned with the state of the *Sangha*, and with the encouragement of Buddhist morality throughout the kingdom through enhancement of Buddhist tradition, provision for teaching, and so on. The pattern of Sinhalese civilization agrees remarkably closely with that of Ashokan India, and both of them with the ideal structure of society which is adumbrated in the discourses of the Buddha.

The extent to which Buddhist tradition permeated the life of the people of Ceylon would have varied from place to place, and from one reign to another. In general it can be said that in Ceylon there was a gradual and steady growth throughout the centuries in the extent and the depth of permeation of popular religious cults and beliefs by Buddhist ideas and values, a process which is still at work today. . . .

Monks as Landlords

One further point which must be mentioned here, however, is the practice which had developed in Ceylon of donating land to monasteries. The land so donated provided the monastery with a regular source of food. The tenants of the land also provided services of various kinds for the monastery. This practice seems to have been established at least as early as the sixth century A.D., for it is admitted in the Ceylon Chronicles that King Aggabodhi I (568–601) made grants of land and monastery-servants to one *Vihara* [monastery], and granted villages to others. This, as Paranavitana points out 'was an innovation which went against the ideals of early Buddhism'. The *Sangha* came to accept such grants as safeguards, ensuring a continuing economic basis for its life in hard times, such as they had in fact experienced under hostile kings, when the continued existence of the *Sangha*, and with it of the *Buddhasasana* [monastic discipline], seemed to be threatened. 'The members of the *Sangha*, however, in order to satisfy their conscience, were expected to refuse when an offer of land grant was made, but to be silent when it was said that the grant was made to the *stupa* [the pagoda-temple]'.

By the time the capital city was shifted from Anuradhapura to Polonnaruva in the eleventh century A.D., the 'biggest landowners were the monasteries, which owned far greater extents of fields, singly and in the aggregate, than any other private owners'. The produce of the land belonged to the monasteries; some of the villagers who worked on the land received a share of this for their own use; others were tenants of cultivable land in return for the services they performed for the monastery.

There are numerous references to such grants of lands in the Ceylon chronicles; the practice of making grants is confirmed by the evidence of inscriptions, some dating from as early as the first century B.C. The practice was not confined to Ceylon, however; grants of land to Buddhist monasteries in India are well attested by inscriptional evidence. The reason given by the donor was almost always the enhancement of his own store of merit. In Ceylon, since land belonging to monasteries was exempt from royal taxation, the permission of the king was required before a would-be donor was allowed to make the transaction. The form of petition which had to be submitted ran as follows 'I am desirous of making this present to the *vihara* for my good, and I pray Your Majesty will permit me, as it is equally for your good. Acceptance of the gift by the *Sangha*, however, as we have seen, implied a tacit recognition of the economic vulnerability of the *Sangha* under the other, older arrangement whereby the *bhikkhus* depended on the generosity of lay people to supply their needs day by day. Under this arrangement, the king, as the leading layman, would usually be one of the most generous donors, and normally there was no real threat to the

Sangha's livelihood. But experience had shown that in troubled times, when the peace of the state was seriously disturbed, the very existence of the *Sangha* could be in danger. Seen from that point of view, the receiving of grants of land by the *Sangha* was wise and provident, but in times of prosperity the possession of such resources of wealth could become a source of corruption and a shifting away from the original perspective.

The Buddhist Calendar and Daily Life

by Robert C. Lester

In the following selection, Robert C. Lester, professor of religious studies at the University of Colorado, examines the Buddhist year in areas of Southeast Asia where Theravada Buddhism is the dominant religion: Burma, Thailand, Laos, and Cambodia, with a focus on the former two. He emphasizes the fact that in these village societies, Buddhism inevitably became intertwined with the rhythms of the agricultural year and with such life-cycle markers as birth and marriage. He also notes that Buddhist faith is intertwined with a belief in spirits dating back to the period before the arrival of Buddhism, and that Buddhist practice in these areas must strike a balance between orthodoxy and these earlier beliefs.

As the surviving remnant of the more traditional, conservative form of Buddhism that took shape in the centuries following the life of the Buddha, Theravada emphasizes reverence toward the three centers of the faith: Buddha (the original enlightened one); dharma (or dhamma, the Buddhist path); and Sangha (the Buddhist community of both monks and laypeople). One of the keys to this reverence is the making of merit, which not only moves one farther along the Buddhist path but is also a sign of the interconnectedness of the Buddhist community. Ordinary people can make merit in many

Robert C. Lester, *Theravada Buddhism in Southeast Asia*. Ann Arbor: University of Michigan Press, 1973. Copyright © 1973 by the University of Michigan. All rights reserved. Reproduced by permission.

ways, such as giving food to monks. Monks and social and political elites, meanwhile, as Lester notes, are thought to possess great merit.

Any act of giving or participation in a ritual which honors the Buddha, from the simple devotion of offering flowers, incense, and candlelight before the Buddha-shrine or of reciting the auspicious marks of the Buddha while fingering beads, to the building or repairing of a monastery is merit-full. . . .

The laity, especially women, make daily food-offerings to the household and yard spirits and to the monks—the former ensuring that the spirits continue to guard and prosper the family and its dwelling; the latter to accumulate merit. They also make daily or frequent incense, flower, and candlelight offerings before the Buddha-image in the home and at the monastery. Four times each month on the moondays (Uposatha) members of the laity (mostly women and older men) will go to the monastery to hear the monks chant, receive the precepts, and listen to a sermon by an elder Bhikkhu [monk]. On these occasions only a few of those present will understand the Pali chants. Some members of the laity will take eight precepts rather than five and remain at the monastery overnight, keeping the basic discipline of the novice. Depending upon the education and the attitude of the preacher, the sermon may be simply a recitation of the Buddha-word or a directive commentary on some contemporary issue. Generally speaking, as with the Roman Catholic Latin mass, the importance of Uposatha to the layman lies not so much in edification by chanting and sermon but in the ritual itself and in being in the presence of and honoring the monk-priest. The Uposatha observance is always closed with a Bhikkhu indicating the merit gained by those who have taken part. It is widely believed that observance of the Uposatha protects one from attack by evil spirits.

The rituals of the life cycle (concerning birth, death, marriage, house-building, etc.) performed in the home or as in the case of a funeral, at the monastery, bring the monk and layman together relative to family solidarity and prosperity. The monks 'bless' the laity and household spirits by their presence, chanting and sprinkling of water, and in return they are fed and gifted by the laity.

Closely associated with most of the life-cycle rituals and also performed on such occasions as ordination, illness, going on or returning from a journey, or honoring a guest is the Sukhwan or Bai Si ceremony. The Bai Si is performed to honor and protect an individual by calling together his vital spirits (*khwan*) and sealing them in his body. The ceremony centers around the *bai si*—a bowl of banana leaves shaped into several-tiered-cones and bearing small balls of cooked rice at their tips. The officiant is usually a layman–former monk; but sometimes on occasion such as illness, a monk. He begins the ceremony by invoking the Buddha, Dhamma, and Sangha, putting the ritual in its proper context. Then he invites, various of the gods, Indra, Brahma, and so forth [pre-Buddhist gods from India or local areas] to take part and to bring wisdom, wealth, beauty, and fertility as may be appropriate to the person for whom the ceremony is being performed. In elaborate ceremonies there follows a circumambulation of the *bai si* by the officiant and others present holding lighted tapers. This done, the Khwan is offered food and called to return to the body of the recipient of the rite. The officiant draws a string around and over the body of the recipient, and then ties it on his wrist. This 'tying of the Khwan' ensures that it will remain in the body and is repeated by other participants in the ceremony. In addition to the Sukhwan there are various other rituals to counteract disease. A group of monks may be invited to chant at the bedside of the ill or special incense, flower, and candlelight offerings may be made before one of especially powerful Buddha-images.

Buddhism and Agriculture

The spirit of the field and the spirit goddess of the rice paddy are propitiated by the farmer at critical points in the agricultural cycle. At the time of first plowing an altar is constructed in the corner of the field and food-offerings are made, usually by the farmer himself. When the rice is 'pregnant' (the grains are beginning to form) it is particularly important to honor the Rice Goddess that she protect the field from malicious spirits and wandering men and animals who might trample the crop. With the Shan [a people of Burma], Thai, Lao, and Khmer, this ritual is essentially a Sukhwan or Bai Si. . . . The rice and field spirits will also be honored at harvest time. Depending on local custom and especially on how good or bad the harvest, this may be a major, all-village festival or a relatively private affair. The monk or former monk may be called upon to chant at any or all of the rice rituals.

Ordination and festival rituals are community affairs. In the largest sense these celebrations cultivate and manifest cultural unity at the village, regional, and national levels. We have seen how an ordination brings merit not only to the ordinand and his family but also to all who by their gifts and presence participate. The power of ordination prior to the rainy season is particularly directed toward heavy rains and fertility of the soil.

As with ordination, the great festivals of the Buddhist year are directed not only to honor and celebrate the Buddha, Dhamma, and Sangha, but also to occasion and celebrate prosperity in worldly affairs. Through these rituals the merit-power of the Buddha and his monks is brought to bear on the spirit-forces controlling the prosperity of the individual, the village, and the nation. The festivals common to all Theravada Southeast Asians are those of the New Year (April), Vesakha (May), Entrance into the Rainy-Season (Vassa), Retreat (June–July), Leaving the Rain Retreat (October), and Kathina (October–November); and the major features of their celebration are everywhere the same.

A Calendar of Buddhist Holidays

The end of the old year, with the advent of the new, is a time for summing up, cleaning up, and starting fresh. The festival gives occasion for honoring the elders and the dead, reflection on the deeds of the past, a symbolic cleansing or washing away of bad deeds (demerit), an actual cleansing of the monastery and Buddha-images, and a rededication to Buddhist values. The new year appropriately begins at the end of the dry season and the beginning of the new life in nature. The pouring of water is not only an honoring of the Buddha, the elders, and the dead but also an offering for plentiful rain and prosperity in the days to come. In Thailand, Laos, and Cambodia, the laity build sand 'pagodas' at the *wat* [temple] or on the bank of the river—each grain of sand represents a demerit, and placing the grains in the *wat* or letting them be washed away by the river symbolizes a cleansing from bad deeds. Bringing sand to the *wat* also serves to renew the floor of the compound. As is the case at all family and community rituals the monks chant blessing-formulas and are offered food by the laity, and the laity renew their precepts. The [chants] are formulas held to have been preached by the Buddha for blessing and protection against evil spirits. The following is frequently employed:

> Therefore may all blessings come to you, may all the devatas [spirits] protect you with the power of the Lord Buddha. May good fortune be yours at all times.
>
> May all blessings come to you, may all the devatas protect you with the power of the Dharma. May good fortune be yours at all times.
>
> May all blessings come to you, may the devatas protect you with the power of the Order.
>
> May good fortune be yours at all times.

It has also become custom throughout the area on New Year's Day to release captive animals—this is most appropriately done by the king and government officials.

[The holiday of] Vesakha, which falls on the last full moon in May, celebrates the birth, enlightenment, and death of the Buddha, all of which occurred during the month of Vesakh-*punnama*. In celebration, the monks are offered special food and a larger number of the laity than usual participate in the Uposatha ritual. A special feature of Vesakha in Burma is the watering of pipal trees—the pipal being the tree under which the Buddha attained enlightenment. Thai, Lao, and Cambodian Buddhists give special honor to the Buddha by processing around the image carrying lighted candles and incense sticks at the conclusion of the Uposatha.

In the period from Vesakha to the entrance into the

Rain Retreat (May–July) the villagers are especially concerned about the timely beginning of the heavy rains. Honoring the Buddha on Vesakha as well as ordaining young men to the monastic order for the coming Rain Retreat generates special power which is brought to bear in hope of rain. Thus, in Laos and parts of Northeast Thailand a rocket festival aimed at rain-making is held on Vesakha itself. Other Thai Buddhists celebrate the same festival at the time of entrance into the Rain Retreat. Burmese Buddhists also have special rain-making rites at this time. The rocket festival provides occasion for friendly competition between groups of monks and laymen in building and firing the rockets and occasion for general merry-making and courting among the young. The rockets are to anger the rain-spirits that they might hurl down torrents of rain and the villagers enjoy a good time before the heavy work in the fields and relatively austere living of the rainy season. . . .

The end of the Rain Retreat is marked by food-offerings to the monks, and lengthy Uposatha. These ceremonies are the beginning of a month-long period of Kathina, the presentation of robes and other gifts to the monks (there is no one day for Kathina). The Kathina offerings to the monks are the most elaborate and most meritorious of their kind made during the Buddhist year—they provide the monk with his clothing and personal supplies for the next twelve months. The offerings are made by the community as a whole and almost every Buddhist participates. The participation of the king and government officials is widely publicized. In connection with the end of the Rain Retreat and the Kathina many Buddhists celebrate a festival of lights. Houses and monasteries are decorated and illuminated and in some areas the laity process around the Buddha-image with lights or float lighted candles on the water, commemorating the moment when the Buddha having gone to the Tusita heaven [an early version of the Buddhist heaven expanded upon in the Mahayana "Pure Land" doctrine] to preach the Dhamma to his mother descended again to the earth.

The month of Kathina is also a time of pilgrimage to famous shrines. Burmese Buddhists may go to the Shwedagon Pagoda in Rangoon or the Shwezigon Pagoda in Tagaung; Thai Buddhists, to Nakom Pathom or the Shrine of the Buddha's Footprint (Phra Buddha Bat) at Saraburi. Offerings at such shrines are especially meritorious.

Many Buddhist villagers complete the yearly ritual cycle with a harvest festival in February or March, making offerings to the spirits accompanied by the prospering and protective chanting of the monks. The forces of nature are to be thanked in prosperity and propitiated in adversity.

The Harmony of Life

There is a ritual rhythm to the life of the Theravada Buddhist. The yearly round of festivals is a ritual cycle coordinated with the agricultural cycle. All of the rituals of the Buddhist way, taken together, promote and express a symphony of life in which all of the various themes—the monk, the layman, the old, the young, the living, the dead, Buddha-power, and spirit-power—are constantly interacting in reciprocity. The monk and the layman are constantly 'meriting' each other. Parents and elders care for the young, performing protective rituals; the young male gives up the pleasures of worldly life, even his sexuality, to bring merit to his elders. The living share merit with the dead believing that the spirits of the dead will aid them or at the least refrain from detrimental activities. The merit of the Buddha and the monk is offered to the spirits that they might prosper the layman's life toward continuation of his ability and capacity to praise the Buddha and support the monk. Merit accrues to the individual in accordance with the extent to which he participates in a merit-full act. This may be understood by the sophisticated in terms of a thought, word, and/or deed occasioning a certain attitude and quality of life within the person, and expressing an attitude and quality of life already present in a person. This may be understood by the less sophisticated in a magical sense, as a thought, word, and/or deed materially conditioning forces in the cosmos which tend his existence in one direction or another. In accordance with either way of understanding, merit may be transferred from one person to another, as one person's action influences the attitude and quality of life of others around him or as material force is magically transferred from one person's holdings to that of others. At the more sophisticated level it is difficult to comprehend how merit can be transferred from the living to the dead; but we must remember that the 'dead' are simply disembodied and are until (and perhaps even though) reincarnated close at hand.

The devout Buddhist may speak only of the long-range effects of merit-making. . . . Nonetheless, he is well aware of, but takes for granted, the manifold short-range implications of merit-making for the social, economic, and political patterns of his society—whether the merit-act is a food-offering to the monk or the construction of a hospital. In the village and to a lesser extent in the urban centers, social status, social mobility, the socialization process, and the economy are importantly conditioned by merit-making. The layman "has practised so as to conquer both worlds; he tastes success both in this world and in the next."

Merit-Making and Social Status

We have indicated the high status and authority enjoyed by the monk and the former monk, not only with respect to ritual affairs but also with respect to the whole gamut of worldly concerns. This status is understood as merit-status. Kings, high government officials, and the wealthy are also considered to have great merit. In general, the more merit a man 'makes', the greater is his social status. The power and prestige which one holds are the result of past merit-making; likewise, the maintenance and enhancement of status depend on continued merit-making. Of course, the presently wealthy and prestigious have greater capacity to make merit than men of little wealth and power—we may say the former have greater social mobility than the latter. We must remember, however, that any male, of age, may become a monk thereby taking on the highest possible status without reference to economic or political power; and, considering the opportunity for an education and for a transvillage awareness open to a member of a nationally oriented monastic order, the monk may return to lay life with the potential for much higher status than he otherwise would have enjoyed. One's merit-potential is his social-mobility potential. In general, the male may enjoy greater social mobility than the female since he can become a monk; the wealthy may enjoy greater social mobility than the poor since they can make greater merit.

Becoming a Monk

by Donald K. Swearer

In all forms of Buddhism it is common for believers to serve as monks. While some choose to devote their entire lives to the monastic path, it is far more common for believers to join monasteries for only a short period of time; joining a monastery is not a lifetime commitment as it is in the Christian world. In Theravada Buddhism people sometimes decide to serve as monks for a period of time in order to have a spiritual retreat, to remind them of the true path to enlightenment in a busy world full of distractions. Others live as monks, forsaking all luxuries and not eating past noon, while still engaged in their everyday lives. The common pattern, however, is for young men to serve as monks for a period of up to a year; thus, monkhood is a kind of coming-of-age ritual. In some areas, in fact, tradition says that a young man who has not served as a monk will have difficulty finding a wife. Potential brides, to use the common term, will not consider him "fully cooked."

The following selection is a description of the process of ordination for monks in Burma, Thailand, Laos, and Cambodia. In it the author, Donald K. Swearer, examines the various incentives and benefits of joining a monastery as well as the importance monkhood plays in the cultures of Theravada countries. He adds that, though it is possible for women to serve in monasteries, it is only in Burma where the status of nuns is anywhere close to that of monks. Swearer is a professor of religion at Swarthmore College.

Ordination into the Theravāda Buddhist monkhood can be interpreted on a variety of levels. From a doctrinal perspective, the monk is a "religious virtuoso"; that is, in seeking ordination monks commit themselves to a lifetime pursuit of the highest goal in Buddhism, *nibbāna* [nirvana], within the context of the monastic order. The Pali term *bhikkhu/bhikkhun* means one who gives up ordinary pursuits of livelihood for a higher goal to become a mendicant or "almsperson." Monks' alms seeking "is not just a means of subsistence, but an outward token that . . . [they] have renounced the world and all its goods and have thrown . . . [themselves] for bare living on the chances of public charity." The *Dhammapāda*, probably the best known of all the Theravāda texts, characterizes the doctrinal ideal of the monk as follows: "the true monk is one whose senses are restrained and who is controlled in body and speech, he is contented with what he receives, is not envious of others and has no thought of himself. Such selflessness is rooted in the Buddha's truth (*dhamma* [*dharma*]) and the monk who dwells in and meditates on the *dhamma* is firmly established in the Truth (*saddhamma*). Such a being is suffused with loving kindness (*mettā*), possesses the cardinal virtues, is refined in conduct, and is filled with a transcendental joy. Confident in the Buddha's teachings, having attained peace and supreme bliss, the monk 'illumines this world like the moon from a cloud.'"

In short, ideal monks are those who seek and attain the truth. Having reached this goal they become morally and spiritually transformed, irradiating the Buddha's *dhamma* for the benefit of humankind. In all Theravāda countries meditation monasteries maintain an environment of peaceful tranquility where men and women pursue the Buddhist ideal of *nibbāna:* the overcoming of suffering, the attainment of equanimity, and insight into the true nature of reality. Although some enter the monastery to seek *nibbāna*, others fall short of this ideal. [Scholar of Buddhism] Melford Spiro analyzed Burmese men's reasons for entering the monkhood into three conscious types—religious motives, the desire to escape the difficulties and miseries of human life, the wish to obtain an easier living—and three unconscious motives—dependency, narcissism, and emotional timidity. Other, somewhat more socially descriptive reasons for entering the monastery include acquiring an education, achieving a higher social status, a response to social custom and pressure, and repayment of a filial debt, especially to one's mother. Before analyzing the ordination ceremony itself, we shall briefly examine some of these motives.

In Burma, Thailand, Laos, and Cambodia monastic tenure varies greatly in length, depending upon the motivation for ordination. Unlike the norm in Western Christianity, becoming a monk may not involve a lifetime commitment, although many noted meditation teachers and scholar-monks may spend their adult life in robes.

In Thailand one of the principal reasons for being ordained is to acquire an education. Among poorer families often children cannot afford to attend school. Ordination as a novice provides for their material needs as well as a basic education. Indeed, if a boy is bright and highly motivated he may complete secondary school as a novice or a monk, graduate from a monastic college, and then earn an advanced degree from a university in another country, such as India. After teaching in a monastery school for several years or serving as an administrator in a larger provincial monastery he will probably disrobe and take a responsible and respected secular job. Although such exploitation of the monastic educational structure siphons off able leadership, it has become standard practice and bears little or no social stigma.

Undoubtedly this pattern of being educated in monastic schools only to leave the order reflects an earlier practice where a young man would be ordained as a novice near the age of puberty, remain in the monastery for one or more years, and then return to lay society. During this period he would receive a rudimentary education, learn the fundamentals of Buddhism, and prepare to lead a responsible life as a lay Buddhist supporter of the monastic order. This particular pattern, still followed in some areas of Southeast Asia, resembles a rite of passage into adulthood. In this sense, the Western parallel to ordination as a Buddhist novice, customarily between the ages of twelve and nineteen, is the rite of confirmation in the Christian tradition and bar and bas mitzvah in the Jewish. Traditionally these ceremonies symbolize full participation in their respective religio-social communities, just as having been ordained a Buddhist monk is considered an essential stage in the passage to mature male adulthood in Thai, Lao, Burmese, or Cambodian society and culture.

The monk takes a vow of celibacy and is expected to minimize material attachments; however, ordinarily monastic tenure does not involve excessive ascetic practice. Theravāda Buddhism in Southeast Asia consistently upholds the time-honored tradition of the Middle Way. In practice, the monk lives a reasonably comfortable life and occupies a respected status in the community. For children of poorer families, in particular, becoming a monk represents a definite improvement in social, and often economic status. For this reason it is not surprising to find that the majority of Theravāda monks in Southeast Asia do, in fact, come from backgrounds of modest means. For instance, at the two monastic colleges in Bangkok, a high percentage of the students were born in northeastern Thailand, the most economically disadvantaged region of the country.

Finally, it should be noted that ordination is perceived as a way of repaying a debt to one's parents, especially one's mother. That one has come into the world, survived infancy, and become a youth results primarily from her care. Within the calculus of meritorious action, one's ordination gains a spiritual benefit for one's parents. The mutual reciprocity characterizing merit making rituals thus becomes part of ordination into the monastic order. A young man survives infancy due to the material benefits provided by his mother and father, by being ordained he returns to them a spiritual boon.

A Public Ceremony

A village ordination in northern Thailand will customarily be held for one or two days and consists of two parts. The first is an animistic ceremony called propitiating the spirits or calling the spirits; the second is ordination into the novitiate, if the candidate is twenty or older, "higher" ordination. The first part of the ceremony may be held in the ordinand's home and will be the occasion for villagewide festivities with as much feasting, drinking, and general merrymaking as the young man's family can afford. The spirit-calling ceremony is conducted by a layman who performs similar roles at weddings, house dedications, and other auspicious or crisis occasions. His earlier life as an ordained monk has prepared him for learning the protocols for these rituals as well as the methods of chanting and preaching. His ritual role differs from that of the monk but rivals it in importance. He often functions as a ritual mediator between the *sangha* [the monastic order] and the laity.

During the ceremony the lay leader performs a ritual in which he "calls" the ordinand's thirty-two spirits (Thai: *khwan*) away from all previous attachment to the pleasures of lay life so the youth will be unswayed and undivided in his pursuit of the monastic life, especially the trials of celibacy. To attract the *khwan* a special offering bowl is prepared. It may be a relatively simple food offering in a lacquer bowl or a much more elaborate symbolic reconstruction of a cosmic tree symbolizing an axial connection between the human and spirit realms. At the conclusion of the ritual, a sacred thread is then tied around the wrists of the ordinand representing the tying of the *khwan* into his body after they have been "called."

Before the spirit-calling ritual begins, the ordinand will be properly prepared for his ordination. His monastic instructor will shave his head and clothe him in a white robe. These acts symbolize the liminality of this life passage ritual, a transition from householder to monk, a neutering of one's previous identity prior to beginning a new life with a new monastic name. They also represent the monk's disregard for the things of this world, including the vanities of personal appearance. At the conclusion of the spirit-calling ritual, the ordinand, his family, friends, and well-wishers form a procession to the monastery compound. In some instances, the young man will be dressed as Prince Siddhattha and will ride a horse to the monastery reenacting the great renunciation of the Lord Buddha. The procession circles the ordination hall three times. Before entering it the ordinand bows before the boundary stone at the front entrance, invoking the Buddha to forgive his sins and to grant him blessings. The sacrality of the ordination hall, hence, the significance of the ordination ceremony, is indicated by the nine boundary stones buried in the ground marking its center and the eight directional points around its perimeter.

Entering the hall, one of the ordinand's friends may play the role of the tempter Māra, pretending to prevent his entrance, or the ordinand may fling a last handful of coins to the well-wishers who have followed him. He approaches the chapter of ten monks seated on the floor in a semicircle in front of a large Buddha image resting on a raised altar at the far end. Bowing to the floor three times before his preceptor senior monk who will conduct the ordination ceremony, the ordinand presents to him gifts of candles, incense, and robes. Professing the Buddha, his teaching (*dhamma*), and the monastic order (*sangha*) to be his refuge, he requests permission three times to enter "the priesthood in the Vinaya-Dhamma of the Blessed One." The preceptor receives the robes, instructs the ordinand in the Three Gems (i.e., Buddha, *dhamma*, and *sangha*), and meditates on the impermanence of the five aggregates of bodily existence until another monk designated as the young man's instructor formally instructs him in the Ten Precepts upheld by all monastic novices: to refrain from taking life, stealing, sexual intercourse, lying, intoxicants, eating at forbidden times, entertainments, bodily adornments, sleeping on comfortable beds, and receiving money. Having taken the precepts, once again the ordinand approaches the preceptor. Now he is assigned to a senior monk as an instructor and given a Pali name. The instructor hangs his begging bowl over his left shoulder, has the young man identify his bowl and three monastic robes, and then questions him on behalf of the entire chapter. His formal queries include "Do you have leprosy?" "Are you a human?" "Are you free of debt?" "Do you have permission from your parents?" Finding him free of impediments, the instructor then presents the ordinand to the *sangha*, requesting that they admit him into the monastic order. Acknowledging their consent by a collective silence, the assembled monks receive the young man into the order as a novice. The ceremony concludes with the preceptor instructing him in the responsibilities of being a monk.

Opportunities and Restrictions for Women and Girls

Among the Southeast Asian Theravāda Buddhist countries, only Burma affords a parallel adolescent life passage ritual for women. The *shinbyu* ceremony includes not only young boys being ordained into the monastic novitiate for a temporary period, but adolescent girls as well. An all day *shinbyu* I witnessed in Mandalay in 1990 included a morning devoted to entertainment.

Men, women, and children crowd into a pavilion constructed to resemble a palace. Over a dozen boys and girls dressed in costumes of princes and princesses sit on a center stage watching several storytellers and mimes entertain the audience. At the conclusion of the entertainment the girls' ears are pierced and the boys' heads are shaved. Afterwards the boys take the vows of a novice monk. Pierced ears symbolize entrance into adult female roles; temporary novitiate ordination represents a similar preparation for a young boy to assume an adult male role in society. Only in Burma do these adolescent life passage rites include both sexes.

Can women in Theravāda Buddhist cultures enter the monastic order and pursue the same spiritual quest as men? The answer is complex. As texts such as the *Therīgathā* (*Songs of the Nuns*) indicate, from a doctrinal perspective both women and men may attain the goal of *nibbāna*. Historically, however, the rules of discipline make clear that the order of women monks is subordinant to that of men. Furthermore, the order of nuns (*bhikkhuni*) endured in India only until circa 456 C.E. and the order may never have reached mainland Southeast Asia. Today orders of renunciant women flourish in Southeast Asia, although technically they are not *bhikkhuni*. In comparison to Thailand, Laos, and Cambodia, women renunciants in Burma enjoy a higher social and spiritual status. Referred to in Burmese as *thilashin* ("one who bears the burden of *sīla* or virtue"), they manage their own monasteries and pursue higher Buddhist studies including Pali. Like male monks, the *thilashin* may collect morning alms donations and may also undergo temporary novitiate ordination similar to their male counterparts. These two practices indicate that in Burma female as well as male renunciants are perceived to represent a religious field of merit. That *thilashin* enjoy a relatively high social and spiritual status is reflected in the participation of girls in the Burmese *shinbyu*. That is, women in Burma have more opportunities to participate in religio-cultural institutions and practices from which they are virtually excluded in Thailand, Laos, and Cambodia.

An Outsider's Observations of Buddhist Life in Burma

by Norma Bixler

In the mid-1960s Norma Bixler joined her husband, Paul, a university librarian, and their son Mark on a two-year sabbatical stay in Rangoon, the capital of the Southeast Asian nation of Burma. The following selection is from her vivid and opinionated personal memoir of those years. In it she describes how Theravada Buddhism, the dominant religion in Burma, is often a highly personalized faith bound closely to individual experiences and concerns, such as the need to build up good karma by doing good works or other forms of merit making. She also touches on the roles of Buddhist monks and on what she perceives as the unusual status of women in Burmese society: Although Theravada Buddhism holds that women are spiritually inferior to men, women hold high-status positions in the home and professionally.

As Bixler implies, Burma is a multiethnic society. The largest percentage of its people are known as Burmans, but there are also substantial minority groups such as the Mons and Karens. It was partly to include such groups that the oppressive military junta, which has governed Burma in recent decades, changed the country's name to Myanmar. In addition, the nation's capital is now officially known as Yangon rather than Rangoon. In any case, Bixler's account is a clear expression of the strength of Theravada traditions even in the twentieth century.

Burmese Buddhists are Theravada Buddhists as are those in Ceylon, Thailand, Cambodia, and Laos. I can listen to the people of any of these lands talk about Buddhism and understand in essence what they are talking about. Many more Buddhists live in Tibet, Vietnam, China, and Japan; but they are all Mahayana Buddhists, divided into many sects, sometimes with more than one sect in a single country. They differ from each other as much as they do from Theravada Buddhists, sometimes even more. Comparatively few Buddhists remain in India.

The Mahayana Buddhists call the others Hinayana Buddhists, and Hinayana means "the lesser vessel." Naturally I've never heard a Theravada Buddhist call himself that. I've read that Theravada Buddhism is "of the mind" and Mahayana Buddhism is "of the heart." Certainly Burmese Buddhists often boast proudly that the Buddha in his teachings foretold all that science has discovered, and that no knowledge was secret from him. Theravada means "the teaching of the elders," and these Buddhists believe that they in their faith hold closest to the teachings of the Buddha himself. I suppose you might call them the Fundamentalists of Buddhism. These teachings have had almost nine centuries to spread through the culture of the Burmese people.

Most Burmese today are Burmans who so dominate the land that they seldom call themselves Burmans. All citizens of Burma are Burmese, but the minority peoples, though they may be large in numbers, still use also their "other" names. Thus, Dr. Paw and his wife [friends from the university] are Burmese but they are also Karens.

The people who gave Theravada Buddhism to Burma are Burmese but they are also Mons. Nine centuries ago, they weren't Burmese at all, and their gift was not freely given.

The Mons then had a powerful kingdom to the east of present-day Rangoon [Yangon]. They'd been in the land now called Burma much longer than the Burmans themselves, they were rich and prosperous and they owned the sacred Pali scriptures of Theravada Buddhism, the Tripitaka.

Anawrahta [1040–1077], first Burman king to step out of legend into history, wanted those scriptures for his people of the Central Plains, and fought the Mon kingdom to get them. He gained much else—the beginning of Burman dominance of the land, secular teachers of the skills from that more-developed society—but the most important spoils of that war were the Tripitaka and Mon monks to teach this faith of peace and tolerance which forbids all killing.

The Buddha was the protestant [reformer] of Hinduism, and what the Burmese learned nine centuries ago, what is today the core of Buddhism, is both like and sharply unlike Hinduism. He taught that all life was suffering and impermanence, that man was bound to the wheel of life by his own desires and greed, and that he will be born again and again, with the quality of each new life determined by his karma, his past life (the Buddhist law of cause and effect) until he frees himself from his desires and by great individual effort reaches Nirvana. These teachings do not differ greatly from Hinduism. But then the differences begin.

A Religion with No Gods

To me the most astonishing difference is that there is no god in Buddhism, while for the Hindus there are many gods, each, the philosophers say, embodying one of the many characteristics of the godhead, so that together they epitomize the godhead.

"We do not believe in God," U Hla Tun [the author's language teacher] told me during one of our Burmese language lessons, where I learned many things besides language. "Ours is really a philosophy, not a religion."

But sometimes the beliefs of a faith's wise men, its theologians, do not seem to seep down to the common people. Of this I feel sure, for I have seen the worshippers on the platforms of pagodas, I have heard their heartfelt prayers and watched them place their offerings of flowers or candles.

If the absence of any god was to me the most surprising difference from Hinduism, the most intelligent is the Buddha's espousal of the Middle Way, his rejection of extremes. In Burma there are no holy men with matted hair and dirty skeletal bodies. The Buddha taught his followers the discipline of the body's desires. A monk does not eat after high noon, he is a chaste man, he does not indulge his body's desires. But having satisfied his body's basic needs, he leaves off thought of it in his search for truth. He must if he is to reach Nirvana.

This Middle Way, this disbelief in extremes, gives a sunniness, a cleanliness to Theravada Buddhism which is a delight to behold. Its basic structure is not baroque, its lines are clean and uncluttered. Like a modern house,

it allows the sun to pour in everywhere, there are no secret spots to which only the few have entry.

I am probably confusing somewhat the structure of
the religion itself with the structure of Burma's pagodas
and the place of those pagodas in the life of the
Burmese. But no matter. I am a woman. Even on the
theme of Buddhism, I could hardly have sought intimate conversations with monks, who are supposed to
lift their fans to cover their faces when they pass a
woman. Nor was I seeking to learn what the wisest
Buddhist believed. For the *ludu*, as the Burmese call the
ordinary man, and therefore for me, the pagodas and
their use grow from the structure of their religion.

Above all else, the pagoda is their symbol, the
pagoda and the saffron-robed monks. A pagoda is not
a temple, a structure which one enters. Pagodas differ
over the world, for the way they are built has always
been a manifestation of the art of the land and its
people. Today in Burma a pagoda is built of bricks, their
angularity smoothed away with concrete. First comes a
stupa, a rounded mound, and beneath the mound are
supposed to be buried sacred relics, preferably a tooth
or a hair of the Buddha. From the mound rises an ever
narrowing spire, and at the top is the *hti* (the Burmese
word for umbrella), often of great price. They say that
the *hti* of the ancient Shwedagon Pagoda [in Rangoon],
gift of King Mindon in 1871, is set with jewels that
even then were worth 62,000 pounds. The large ruby
which [poet and university librarian] U Thein Han told
me glowed on a moonless night is on that *hti*. The concrete of the pagoda can be covered with whitewash or
on a very important pagoda, like the Shwedagon, the
whole can be surfaced with gold leaf. But whether
white and serene or glittering and majestic, the spires

of pagodas dominated almost every landscape we saw in Burma.

A pagoda can be built anywhere. We saw them in fields, on hills, literally anywhere, and wherever erected, the building brings great merit to the builder. This merit will not in the least help him toward his goal of reaching Nirvana, but it can affect his karma, and his next life may be more pleasant or more holy for the building.

Pagodas are still being built. On the promontory of a hill along the road from Mandalay north to Maymyo stood a new one we liked especially. It was not large, not too blatantly modern, and it stood alone and serene on that promontory, looking out over a valley, some of its whitewash tinted a pale blue, its four Buddhas in four niches at the compass points in the stupa.

Another new one stands on the Shwedagon platform among its elders. It is truly modern, though it makes a bow to the old in its bas-relief, which is a faint reminder of the Khmer art at Angkor Wat [in Cambodia]. I hope it gains its builder much merit but in that ancient place it hurts the eye of the beholder.

The Temple Environment

Main pagodas are built on platforms, often of great size, and raised high in the air, so that one approaches them from any of their four entrances by long flights of stairs. Here merchants may have small stalls which sell, appropriately, flowers, candles, incense, and, more confusingly, brass spoons and household irons, food, knives, drums, gongs, and other muscial instruments. Certain things we always bought at the Shwedagon, and while we took off our sandals before we started up the stairs because we were on sacred ground, our purchases were completely secular.

On the platform itself, usually paved with flagstones, stands most importantly the pagoda. But there are also innumerable shrines or altars, each with a statue of the Buddha, or perhaps many statues side by side. Rest shelters are there for pilgrims, perhaps a small museum if the pagoda is a very old one, perhaps bells, like the ones at the Shwedagon, great bells without clappers, which cannot ring but are struck by a wooden mallet. There will also be space, just space, open and empty, where a monk may sleep, or a family on a pagoda visit, cook rice and spread food to eat. Before the shrines, supplicants kneel quietly, their hands folded, meditating on the Buddha's teachings.

In Burma no services are held as a Western churchgoer knows them. There is a Buddhist Sabbath, although, because the calendar is lunar, it does not always fall on the same day of the week; and there are special festival days. On any of these, it is particularly fitting that a Buddhist go to the pagoda. But he goes at any hour on any day. When Mark [the author's teenage son] joined a group of university students going on a picnic, it was to Pegu they went, sixty miles from Rangoon. There at the Shwe Maw Daw Pagoda, they prepared their food and ate, talked and rested before they started their long drive back. They worshipped, too—no, not worshipped, if the philosophers are correct, but they knelt before the Buddha and meditated. But they did not go to Pegu to meditate at the pagoda; they went to Pegu and the pagoda as university students on a picnic.

The sunny openness of the pagoda platform to which all visitors are welcome may mirror another difference from Hinduism, the lack of caste. Brahmins are the caste of the wise men, but in Burma the *phongyis*, the monks, who are the priests of the nation, may be sons of the minister or sons of the poorest peasant. Even in the day of the king there was democracy in the *phongyi* monastery. Each boy customarily becomes a monk for a while and his *shinbyu*, his ordination, is both a gay and a solemn occasion, a kind of coming-of-age rite.

We passed *shinbyu* processions occasionally when we were driving in the country. The procession was gay, but the young boy in his make-believe-prince costume, being led to the monastery astride a Burmese pony with a make-believe-prince umbrella held over his head, always looked big-eyed, solemn, a little scared. At the monastery, he would trade these make-believe riches for the monk's saffron robe and begging bowl, as a visible sign that he was forsaking the wealth of the secular world for the poverty of a *phongyi*. A boy like this may remain in the monastery if he wishes for the rest of his life, or he may leave the order, returning for intervals of a week or a month during his manhood. No one asks questions. Especially for the week of the Water Festival, just before the monsoons and the beginning of the Buddhist Lent, men return. Perhaps this is only because there is time then, for government offices, schools, and many businesses are closed. The next week, the shaved head of the one-time monk behind his desk or classroom lectern occasions no comment. It is quite natural.

Because no one asks questions, monasteries may provide shelter to the less devout. The Caretaker government raided one monastery in Rangoon, an unheard-of procedure; criticism, however, was rather muffled, since the catch included several known Communist insurgent leaders and a wanted murderer.

Another kind of refugee must also seek shelter in Rangoon monasteries, the poor would-be scholar. My first Burmese lessons were at the Burma-America Institute. As I arrived, English-language pupils were just leaving, among them many monks, a little too old for the customary novice, yet still quite young. When the results of university entrance examinations were posted on the big bulletin board at the doors to Convocation Hall (and these included examinations in English), would-be students crowded about thickly; among them, again, were many in the saffron robe. If they were successful in the examinations, they would doff the robe. *Phongyis* might study, but different subjects in a different school.

Theravada Buddhism is an individualistic philosophy, or religion, call it what you will. It isn't only that no priest stands between a Buddhist and his salvation, or that each man can become a priest at will. It is something much more profound.

Buddhism and Christianity

When U Hla Tun and I talked about Buddhism, we never compared it with Hinduism. But he did compare it for me with Christianity. A graduate of St. Paul's, the best English high school in Burma, he felt he knew what he was talking about.

"In your religion, Christ died to save you. The responsibility is not yours. But our religion is stronger than yours. For our salvation is solely an individual responsibility. Each of us must help himself."

A *phongyi* is a Buddhist so devout that he has resolved to seek Enlightenment, to reach Nirvana in this present life, or come as close to it as he can. He will beg for his food each morning because he has vowed poverty, because begging helps to efface self and keep him humble, because it gives the lay Buddhist an opportunity to gain merit by the giving of the food.

But he need serve the layman in no other way, he is not their priest as we think of a priest. Still, most *phongyis* do assume other responsibilities. They do not officiate at weddings, which are based on the ephemeral emotions of this world, but they do preside at funerals. Many teach in the *phongyi chaungs*, expound the scriptures to devout laymen, and especially in the villages where they are closer to the people, often give spiritual guidance for a secular world. But no monk is required to do these things.

He spends his days in study of the sacred scriptures and in meditation, deep concentration on the teachings of the Buddha, profound beyond what any layman can achieve or even comprehend. His goal is an individual one, not a social one. He seeks Nirvana, and just as U Hla Tun said, each must depend on himself. But the law of karma works for him just as it does for everyone else.

I never talked to U Hla Tun about the monks who begged from me, or the young monks at the movies. Religion and politics are abrasive subjects for argument everywhere, but there is a particular rudeness when a guest seems to discredit his host's beliefs in either. So my questions of him and my other friends were always learning questions; I avoided either questions or statements which seemed critical. Nevertheless, as I learned about the monk's role from them, I learned also to understand most of the contradictions which had puzzled me.

As a former monk himself, Aung Tin [the author's local driver] was filled with scorn at the sight of a yellow robe at a movie. He knew quite well the rules of the *Sangha* [monastic community]. A monk who begged for money would have made another Burmese sad. But neither would brood over it. Karma, in good time and another life, would punish the small minority of monks who dishonored the robe. Their reaction, like the monk's act, was an individual one, not a social one.

Burmese did tell me that in the days of the kings, the *Sangha* was not as undisciplined. Then at the court there was a single *phongyi* of great learning and holiness who was the head of the order. Today there is only the *Sasana*, a part of the Ministry of Religion and Culture, where leading monks, government officials, and devout laymen join in discussing questions affecting Buddhism. But it isn't the same authority.

My friends told me, too, that sometimes in villages such questions were resolved differently. After all, a monk is a symbol of this faith, an example to the laity. If he sets a bad example in a small community, the villagers sometimes discipline him themselves. They decline to give him food when he comes to beg. Of course the knife cuts both ways. The monk may also cover his begging bowl and refuse to accept food from a villager who flagrantly disobeys the five basic precepts.

Most laymen are far more concerned with their karma than with Nirvana. Enlightenment is many lives away; Nirvana is without precise definition. The Buddha presumably said that he did not answer all the questions of man, though he knew the answers, because some answers the finite mind was not ready to comprehend. So it is with Nirvana. But death will come with certainty, and with equal certainty will come rebirth.

Karma and Merit Making

The scholars insist the Buddha did not teach that each rebirth is of the same self, but the folklore of Burma is full of stories of children who in their early years can remember their last life, can recognize in their present life the people and the places of their past.

One pleasant tale is of a monk who came upon a small village which had no monastery, though nearby grew a fine grove of trees. He looked upon the trees, nodded in satisfaction, and said to the villagers: "I planted these trees several lives ago when they were very small. Now they are big and strong. Come, help me cut them down and make them into lumber and we will build a monastery, just as I planned when I planted the trees, long ago."

Besides, there are the *Jataka* stories of all the lives the Buddha lived, some of them as an animal, before he reached Enlightenment and became the Buddha. Our friends at the Pyinmana Agricultural Institute had brought in large American pigs to upgrade the Burmese stock. Though the Burmese willingly took setting eggs from the big American hens, they showed marked disinterest in the white piglets. Finally the Americans learned that the Buddha in one of his incarnations had been a white pig. They exchanged their large white pigs for large black pigs, and these the Burmese accepted.

With this strong sense of lives past and lives to come, karma is of natural importance. If a man lives well in this life, he can expect his next life to give him greater opportunities for gaining merit. He may even be more handsome, more prosperous.

Meanwhile, in this life, he must at the very least obey the five basic precepts. But they are not too difficult. One does not kill anything, or take that which is not given, or lie, or commit adultery, or drink alcohol. Merit is to be gained by feeding the *phongyis*, by giving *shinbyus* for boys too poor to have proper ones, by giving gifts to monasteries or pagodas. Indeed all such giving is to be limited only by one's wealth, and all not only gain merit for the giver and help to insure one's next life, but give one status in one's present society.

This religion makes women somewhat second-class devotees. No woman may reach Nirvana until she has first been born a man, and being therefore less holy, Buddhist nuns, of whom there are a few, receive almost none of the reverence due a Buddhist monk. The body is to be respected in declining value from the head to the toe, and the man to be more respected than the woman. No woman would toss her *longyi* (her skirt) across her man's sleeping mat where his head has lain; little boys wear little knitted caps on outings even in warm weather, and women are never to rumple the hair of even the most charming small Burmese male. Fortunately I learned this very early or the gay youngster who brought me roses from the compound next door would have led me inevitably to break a taboo.

The Puzzling Status of Women

Burmese women readily grant this secondary religious role but insist that to them it is quite unimportant and that they play the role willingly with full sense of equality in their society. For Burma's women are free and unveiled, to be met in the marketplace, the village center, the professions of the cities. They keep their own names after marriage, divorce is easy, though not frequent, property is shared equally by husband and wife. Almost every other woman in Burma earned at least some small sum through her own endeavors, whether it was the produce she took to market, the silk she wove, or the stall she operated in the bazaar. Few professional women retire after marriage or the birth of their children.

For a country lying between India and China where the role of women has been quite different, this puzzled me, but no Burmese could explain it. Equally puzzling, in some ways, was the devotion of the woman Buddhist. Buddhism would seem to be a man's religious world. But women were, if anything, more devout. They were the ones who fed the monks each morning, sometimes, especially in the villages, with more choice food than they fed their families. They were most regular in their pagoda visits, and a mother's heart would have broken if her son did not have his *shinbyu* with the proper richness and ceremony.

CHAPTER 3

*The Greater Path:
Mahayana Buddhism
in East Asia*

Buddhism Adjusts to Chinese Life and Thought

by Daniel L. Overmyer

Buddhism entered China slowly over centuries beginning in the first century A.D., taken there by wandering monks traveling overland from India. In many ways the opposite of Confucianism, the philosophy of the Chinese ruling class based on ritual and earthly order, Buddhism became widespread only during the era of the so-called Six Dynasties (221–586), when China had no centralized government to resist it. In the following selection, religious scholar Daniel L. Overmyer describes how Buddhism became the religion of many ordinary people in China as well as a faith appealing to certain social elites. For ordinary people, Overmyer notes, Pure Land Buddhism, with its promise of an appealing afterlife, had the greatest attraction. Pure Land Buddhism was also flexible enough to accommodate the numerous Chinese gods or spirits that predated the arrival of Buddhism; now these spirits, such as Kuan Yin, the Chinese "goddess of mercy," could be described as bodhisattvas, or enlightened souls who chose to remain in the world to help people rather than attain nirvana and cease being reborn. Social elites, meanwhile, were drawn to the more rigorous Ch'an school, which offered enlightenment in this lifetime rather than an afterlife.

Overmyer also notes that Buddhism often faced resistance from adherents to both Confucianism and Taoism (also known as Daoism), philosophies and religions that emerged in the fifth and fourth centuries B.C. that had become central to China's culture. Confucians disliked what they saw as Buddhism's abstraction and other-worldly emphasis. Taoists, however, may have simply felt threatened by this powerful faith that in many respects was close to their own. Taoists believe, for instance, in the importance of meditation and in the search for the proper path to contentment, or the Tao. As the decades passed, however, and despite periods of persecution, Buddhism came to join Confucianism and Taoism as the foundations of traditional Chinese culture.

Daniel L. Overmyer is emeritus professor of religious studies at the University of British Columbia in Canada.

Indian Buddhists came to regard the Buddha as a super-human being whose teachings are eternally true. Since they believed that every person had lived many lifetimes in different places, it was natural to believe that Sakya-muni [Gautama, founder of Buddhism] had been through many life cycles before the rebirth in which he attained enlightenment. Some Indian thinkers had long maintained that our universe is just one of many, and that each universe has a history of birth, growth, and decline, a view quite similar to that of modern astronomy. So it was that Buddhists began to say that in fact there were many Buddhas, one for each of the myriad universes, yet all preaching the same basic wisdom. As each universe went through cycles of death and rebirth, new Buddhas appeared to resume the teaching anew, because it too declined in power and had to be revived. Our world is the same; even now it is becoming more difficult to communicate Sakyamuni's teaching because people are ignorant and stubborn, and a new Buddha-to-be—Maitreya, the future Buddha—is waiting in heaven to come to earth and start Buddhism all over again.

The combination of these ideas led to the belief that even in our universe there are many Buddhas, each in his own land or realm, each representing a particular Buddhist virtue, such as wisdom or compassion. Though Sakyamuni is the Buddha of our particular historical cycle, these other celestial Buddhas are available to help reinforce his teaching. The most popular of them is Amitabha, the Buddha of compassion who presides over a paradise, or "Pure Land," far to the west. Those who believe in him, meditate upon him, and pray for his aid will be saved and go to his paradise at death. There they will be surrounded by the Buddha's influence and teaching and easily attain enlightenment. This belief was appealing to many people because it promised a better afterlife than going to purgatory or just being reborn on earth. It was also more specific than nirvana and gave people more to look forward to.

The Promises of Pure Land Buddhism

Indian scriptures describing Amitabha's paradise were translated into Chinese by the third century A.D., and by the sixth century some Chinese monks began to base their whole message on this belief, telling people that if they just called out Amitabha's name in faith they would be saved. There was no need for meditation or studying philosophy, or even being able to read; just faith and devotion were enough. These Buddhist evangelists went around preaching and organizing groups of Amitabha worshipers, and people responded by the tens of thousands. By the seventh century Pure Land was the most popular form of Buddhism in China, and it remains so to this day, in both China and Japan (which it reached in the ninth century). The appeal of this hope for paradise is easy to understand, because the Pure Land is described in Buddhist scriptures as a wonderful place indeed. In one book the Buddha tells his disciple Ananda that the Pure Land (Sukhavati in Sanskrit), is

> the world system of the Lord Amitabha, rich and prosperous, comfortable, fertile, delightful and crowded with many Gods and men. And in this world system, Ananda, there are no hells, no animals, no ghosts, no Asuras [demons] and none of the inauspicious places of rebirth.
>
> . . .
>
> And that world system Sukhavati, Ananda, emits many fragrant odours, it is rich in a great variety of flowers and fruits, adorned with jewel trees, which are frequented by flocks of various birds with sweet voices. . . . And these jewel trees, Ananda, have various colours, many colours, many hundreds of thousands of colours. They are variously composed of the seven precious things, in varying combinations, i.e., of gold, silver, beryl, crystal, coral, red pearls or emerald.
>
> . . .
>
> And many kinds of river flow along in this world system Sukhavati. There are great rivers there, one mile broad, and up to fifty miles broad and twelve miles deep. And all these rivers flow along calmly, their water is fragrant with manifold agreeable odours, in them there are bunches of flowers to which various jewels adhere, and they resound with various sweet sounds.

In this paradise people get whatever they wish for, be it music, fine food, clothing, jewels, or palaces. They look and live like gods. But most important, in the Pure

Land they constantly hear the Buddha's teaching, so that it is easy for them to attain enlightenment, never more to be reborn on earth. Believers are assured that nowhere in this wonderful place

> does one hear of anything unwholesome, nowhere of the hindrances, nowhere of the states of punishment, the states of woe and the bad destinies, nowhere of suffering. Even of feelings which are neither pleasant nor unpleasant one does not hear here, how much less of suffering! And that, Ananda, is the reason why this world-system is called the "Happy Land."

All this is available to those who sincerely believe in the Buddha and his power.

The Challenges of Chan, or Zen, Buddhism

Pure Land Buddhism was fine for ordinary people, but it became a mass movement that some of the more individualistic and intellectual did not respond to. They were concerned for enlightenment now in this life and argued that however beautiful a Pure Land was, it was still not nirvana, the ultimate peace and clarity of mind. Some of them also felt that by the seventh and eight centuries [the height of China's Tang dynasty] Buddhism had become *too* successful. There were thousands of monasteries, many of them wealthy, with lots of land, servants, and golden images donated by rich merchants and officials. By this time there had been several Buddhist emperors who gave money and official status to monasteries and expected the monks to support them in return. Buddhism was becoming a new form of Chinese state religion, which some more dedicated monks thought distracted people from the real point of their faith: finding a new level of awareness and acceptance within. By the seventh century some reforming monks began a movement back to quiet meditation as the central practice of Buddhism. Before long, these monks were considered to be the founders of a new school of Buddhism, the meditation school, or *Chan*, a word that in Japanese is pronounced "*Zen.*" This school soon became quite popular among pious officials and merchants, but it never had the mass appeal of Pure Land, because the Chan path to salvation took more time and hard work. In part it was a return to the self-enlightenment that had been advocated by Sakyamuni himself a thousand years earlier. Some Chan leaders, feeling that Buddhism had become too worldy and materialistic, rejected images and scriptures and spent their lives meditating in small isolated monasteries, but most Chan people felt that images and scriptures were useful reminders of Buddhist truth as long as one did not become attached to them and remembered that the potential for enlightenment was inside every person. Their slogan was: "Become a Buddha yourself by realizing your own inner potential." It is not surprising that it is this form of Buddhism that has had the most appeal in North America and Europe, because it sounds similar to our own ideas of self-development. Listen, for example, to some passages from the teachings of the Chan masters:

> Within your own natures the ten thousand things will all appear, for all things of themselves are within your own nature. Given a name, this is the pure . . . Buddha.
>
> . . .
>
> Good friends, when I say "I vow to save all sentient beings everywhere," it is not that I will save you, but that sentient beings, each with their own natures, must save themselves. What is meant by "saving yourselves with your own natures"? Despite heterodox views, passions, ignorance, and delusions, in your own physical bodies you have in yourselves the attrib-

utes of inherent enlightenment, so that with correct views you can be saved. If you are awakened to correct views, the wisdom of *prajna* will wipe away ignorance and delusion and you all will save yourselves.

. . .

Good friends, each of you must observe well for himself. Do not mistakenly use your minds! The sutras say to take refuge in the Buddha within yourselves; they do not say to rely on other Buddhas. If you do not rely upon your own natures, there is nothing else on which to rely.

Prajna is a Sanskrit term for the wisdom of the enlightened mind, which sees things as they really are, without fear or illusion. It is this wisdom that makes a Buddha a Buddha; since we can also attain such enlightenment, we can become Buddhas too. All the potential for salvation is in our own minds.

Resistance from Traditionalists

Even though various forms of Buddhism became very popular during the Tang dynasty, there were always some Daoists and Confucians who did not like it and who several times convinced rulers to make Buddhism illegal, confiscate monasteries, and force monks and nuns to return home. Most of these persecutions did not last long, but finally, in A.D. 844–845, a Daoist emperor forced thousands of monasteries to close and made most of the monks and nuns give up their religious vocations. This suppression of Buddhism was the most devastating of all. Then as now the Chinese government claimed complete authority over religion as well as politics and society. As a result of this nationwide persecution, many of the most important monasteries were ruined, and, with them, the schools of Buddhist study and philosophy they supported. Eventually the law was changed again, and Buddhism was allowed to rebuild, but now there were only two schools left, Chan and Pure Land, both of which survived because of their popular support. Since then, they have been the dominant forms of Buddhism in all of east Asia. The most important reason for their success in China is that they both were developed there by Chinese monks who knew what their people wanted—a religious hope that was simple, direct, and practical, and that in the case of Pure Land could be carried out in the midst of ordinary social life. Even Chan monks developed forms of meditation that could be practiced by merchants and officials at home. Chan leaders also taught that the eternal truth of Buddhism was the same as the cosmic Dao, so that one could seek enlightenment amid the beauties of nature. So it was that Buddhism too found its place in the Chinese view of the world.

The Devotion of Two Chinese Nuns

by Shih Pao-ch'ang

From its earliest days, Buddhism has provided room for female as well as male devotees in its monastic orders. Indeed, the first *bhikkuni*, or Buddhist nun, was Prajapati, the original Buddha's aunt. According to the stories of the original Sangha, or Buddhist community, the Buddha was convinced to allow Prajapati to join by his cousin, Ananda, who told the Buddha that it might be possible for women as well as men to understand the Buddhist path to enlightenment. Ananda's argument was unusual for the period, a time when it was widely believed that women were subordinate to men and incapable of deep intellectual or spiritual understanding. The Buddha, however, was convinced, and from that point on most sects of Buddhism allowed for nuns as well as monks, although in general nuns had to accept lesser positions in monasteries. As with other aspects of these emerging sects, the status of nuns was greatly affected by local conditions and views of women's roles.

The following selection is from a collection of biographies of Chinese Buddhist nuns who lived during the fourth through sixth centuries, when Buddhism was taking hold in China. The volume is attributed to Shih

Pao-ch'ang, a monk living in the sixth century. The stories of Seng-kuo and Ching-ch'eng demonstrate that women could not only serve as nuns but also achieve high levels of enlightenment. They also reflect how Buddhism became combined with certain elements of Chinese culture by emphasizing, for instance, worldly cleverness and practicality, qualities highly valued in traditional China. Indeed, the biographies themselves serve as lessons, a reflection of the faith in traditional China that one learns best by studying examples of past lives and accomplishments.

Seng-Kuo

The nun Seng-kuo (Fruit of the Sangha) (b. 408) of Kuang-ling.

Seng-kuo's secular surname was Chao; her given name was Fa-yu. Her family was originally from Hsiu-wu in Chi Commandery [in north China].

Because she had established genuine faith during a former life, pure devotion was natural to her in her present life, and, even when she was an infant at breast, she did not transgress the monastic rule of not eating after mid-day. Her father and mother both marveled at this. When Seng-kuo grew up, although she was of one mind about what she wanted to do, the karmic obstructions were mixed and multiform. Therefore she was twenty-seven years old before she was able to leave the household life, at which time she became a disciple of the nun Huits'ung of Kuang-ling [on the north bank of the Yangtze River northeast of the capital]. Seng-kuo cultivated an intelligent and solid observance of the monastic regulations, and her meditative practice was so free from distractions that each time she entered into concentration she continued thus from dusk to dawn. Stretching in spirit to the pure realm of the divine, her body stayed behind looking as lifeless as dry wood, but some of her disciples of shallow understanding were doubtful of her yogic ability.

In the sixth year of the *yüan-chia* reign period (429), a foreign boat captain named Nan-t'i brought some Buddhist nuns from Sri Lanka to the capital of the Sung dynasty. The Sri Lankan nuns stayed at Luminous Blessings Convent.

Not long after taking up residence there, they asked Seng-kuo, "Before we came to this country, had foreign nuns ever been here?"

She replied, "No, there have not been any."

They asked again, ["If that is the case] how did the Chinese women who became nuns receive the monastic obligations from both the Assembly of Monks and the Assembly of Nuns [as they are required to do according to the rules?]"

Seng-kuo replied, "They received the obligations only from the Assembly of Monks."

"Those women who went through the ritual of entering the monastic life began the reception of the monastic obligations. This reception was an expedient to cause people to have great respect for the monastic life. Our eminent model for this expedient is the Buddha's own stepmother, Mahāprajāpatī, who was deemed to have accepted the full monastic obligation by taking on herself, and therefore for all women for all time, the eight special prohibitions incumbent on women wanting to lead the monastic life. [These she accepted from the Buddha only.] The five hundred women of the Buddha's clan who also left the household life at the same time as

Mahāprajāpatī considered her as their instructor."

Although Seng-kuo agreed, she herself had a few doubts [about the validity of the rituals that had been observed in China regarding women leaving the house-

Modern-day bhikkunis, *Buddhist nuns, pray at a Tibetan nunnery.*
Buddhism allows women as well as men to practice the monastic lifestyle.

hold life]. Therefore she asked the central Asian missionary monk Gunavarman [who was an expert on the subject]. He agreed with her understanding of the situation.

She further inquired of him, "Is it possible to go through the ritual [of accepting the full monastic obligation] a second time?"

Gunavarman replied, "[The Buddhist threefold action of] morality, meditation, and wisdom progresses from the slight to the obvious. Therefore, receiving the monastic obligations a second time is of greater benefit than receiving them only once."

[Four years later] in the tenth year (433), Nan-t'i, the ship captain, brought eleven more nuns from Sri Lanka, including one named Tessara. The first group of nuns, who by this time had become fluent in Chinese, requested the Indian missionary monk Sanghavarman to preside over the ritual for bestowing the monastic rules on women at the ceremonial platform in Southern Grove Monastery. That day more than three hundred women accepted once again the full monastic obligation [this time from both the Assembly of Monks and the Assembly of Nuns].

One time, in the eighteenth year (441), when she was thirty-four years old, Seng-kuo sat in meditation for a whole day. [Because she had sat so long and her body was still and lifeless like dry wood] the administrator of the meditation hall tried to rouse her but could not and therefore said that she had died. Alarmed, she summoned the other officers of the convent who, on examining Seng-kuo, perceived that her body was cold and stiff. Her breath was so slight as to be unnoticed, and they were on the point of carrying her away when she opened her eyes and talked and laughed like her usual self. Thereupon, those foolish ones [who had doubted her] were startled into accepting her achievements in meditation.

It is not known how or when she died.

Ching-Ch'eng

The nun Ching-ch'eng (Measure of Quietude) of Bamboo Grove Convent in Tung-hsiang of Shan-yang [north of the capital on the south bank of the Huai River].

Ching-ch'eng's secular surname was Liu; her given name was Sheng. Her family was originally from Ch'iao Commandery [in the Huai River valley].

Besides Ching-ch'eng's stringent practice of the monastic rules, she was also able to chant 450,000 words of scripture. The mountain grove next to the convent had no clamor or distractions, and in that fine location Ching-ch'eng's mind roamed in the silence of meditation, cutting off forever worldly corruption and trouble.

Once a man lost an ox and went searching for it. By nightfall he had come to the mountain where he saw the bright glare of firelight in the convent grove, but, when he approached it, the light disappeared.

A tiger often followed Ching-ch'eng in her comings and goings, and, when she sat in meditation, the tiger settled down nearby. If one of the nuns in the convent did not make a timely confession of an offence she had committed against the rules, the tiger would be angry, but, after she confessed, the tiger would be pleased.

Later, when Ching-ch'eng came out for a brief while from her seclusion on the mountain, on the way she encountered a woman from the north. They greeted one another without engaging in the usual formalities and were as pleased and happy as old friends. The woman's name was Ch'iu Wen-chiang, and she was originally from Po-p'ing [in northeast China, in the border region between the non-Chinese dynasty in the north and the Chinese dynasty in the south]. Ch'iu Wen-chiang's character was such that she particularly liked the Buddhist teaching. She had heard that in the south the Way was flourishing, and, when she was able to get across the frontier, she went as a refugee to this territory, where she became a nun.

Together with Ching-ch'eng, Ch'iu Wen-chiang led an austere life in the convent. Neither of the two women would eat millet or rice but instead ate only sesame and mountain thistles. Their reputation for strict asceticism became known in the capital of the northern barbarians who called the women sages and from afar summoned them with greetings of welcome. The two women, however, did not like the frontier region, and therefore they proceeded to besmirch their own reputation by being, as [(Chinese philosopher) Confucius recommended] "bold in action while conciliatory in speech" when in a country where the Way does not prevail. The barbarian host had prepared for them a meal of fine delicacies, which the women immediately gobbled right down, paying no attention to manners. Because of this the ruler lost his former respect for them and detained them no longer. Ching-ch'eng and Wen-chiang returned to their convent.

Ching-ch'eng was ninety-three years old, free from any malady, when she died.

Buddhism in Japan

by H. Byron Earhart

Buddhism arrived in Japan after it had taken hold in neighboring China and Korea in the fifth and sixth centuries. Indeed, it formed a large part of the cultural heritage that Japan gained from China, with Korea as the frequent intermediary, in these centuries and after, a heritage that in addition to Buddhism included the Confucian school of social philosophy and administration and the Chinese written language. At first, when the Japanese empire was consolidated during the so-called Nara period (710–784), Buddhism was generally a religion of aristocratic and warrior elites, and Nara monks and scholars correspondingly played a large role in politics. Among the early schools of importance were Tendai, a sect of monks trained at a vast monastery on Mount Hiei near Kyoto, many of whom went on to work for the state, and Shingon, which emphasized elaborate rituals and the arts.

Buddhism spread to a wider population in Japan mostly due to two other sects that also originated in China, Pure Land and Zen, which had arrived earlier but became widespread during the Kamakura period (1192–1338). These two schools of Buddhism are the subject of the following selection. Author H. Byron Earhart examines how Pure Land Buddhism offered the promise of salvation to ordinary people who lacked the time, wealth, or opportunity to devote their lives to meditation and ritual. He also examines the popular and often misunderstood Zen school, which itself subdivided into different sects and had a major influence on Japanese art and aesthetics. Earhart taught religion at Western Michigan University.

The term "Pure Land" (or "Pure Realm") is a translation of the Japanese term *Jodo*. It can refer to one particular group of Buddhist sects, the Pure Land sects, but in a broader sense it refers to the Pure Land of Amida in the Buddhist pantheon. Amida (Amitabha or Amitayus in Sanskrit) was an important Buddha even in Indian Buddhism and became one of the most important objects of Buddhist devotion in China. Amida has compassion on and wants to save all human beings. To rescue them Amida brings humans to the Buddhist realm called the Pure Land. All people can avail themselves of Amida's saving grace simply by invoking or chanting the name of Amida. In Japan this practice is known as *nembutsu:* The actual phrase is *namu Amida* or *namu Amida Butsu*, meaning "I put my faith in Amida Buddha." Originally the *nembutsu* meant meditation on Amida, but the element of meditation was soon replaced by fervent devotion and endless repetition. The development of the Pure Land sects expressed the shift from meditation to faith. In China and then in Japan the cult of Amida became closely associated with memorials for the dead.

The simplicity of faith in Amida helped spread this cult throughout the land. Although all people yearned for their own salvation and the repose of their ancestors, only a few could spend the time and money for Shingon rituals and Tendai meditation [earlier, more scholastic sects]. Furthermore, no comprehension of subtle doctrines was required in Pure Land Buddhism. The founders of the Pure Land sects were thoroughly trained in the monasteries of Hieizan [Mount Hiei] and elsewhere, but they emphasized the availability of salvation for even illiterate peasants. Amida Buddhism did not win the day because people chose to follow Pure Land doctrine instead of Tendai and Shingon doctrine. It was not a matter of choosing one intellectual system over another so much as it was a matter of choosing popular devotion to Amida over the former Buddhist systems. Faith in Amida became more important for the people than all the earlier Buddhist movements combined—the philosophical systems of Nara Buddhism, the rituals of Shingon, and the meditation of Tendai. . . .

Amidism is one of the most pervasive of all religious movements within Japanese history. Faith in Amida preceded the founding of the Pure Land sects and overflowed the boundaries of those sects. The *nembutsu* was something that people accepted and practiced regardless of their own temple affiliation. Amida was responsive to all who called on the name of Amida, and men and women and children looked to Amida for help in time of need. It is said that on medieval battlefields the dying warriors sent up their loud pleas for Amida to take them to the Pure Land.

Pure Land priests were active both in spreading Buddhist faith in the heart of the cities and in building temples in rural areas. Even the pattern of temple organization was an innovation to Japanese Buddhism. In the past, temples had been founded and maintained mainly by government sponsorship. Shinran gathered together practitioners of the *nembutsu*, along the lines of popularly organized congregations. Rennyo and others later solidified this network of believers into a tight organizational system. It is no accident that Pure Land groups in general and Jodo Shinshu in particular possess one of the largest memberships and are among the most tightly organized of all Japanese Buddhist groups. . . .

The Zen Sects: Enlightenment Through Meditation

Zen is the most publicized but not necessarily the most understood aspect of Japanese Buddhism. Many Westerners have been led to believe that Zen tells the whole story of Japanese Buddhism and the Japanese spirit. In this short work, the treatment of Zen must be limited to its role in Japanese religious history. There is already a vast popular literature for Westerners dealing with contemporary Zen as a personal philosophy of life, to which the reader may refer. However, to understand Zen historically, we must recognize that in Japan it first rose to prominence during the Kamakura period. Therefore, it existed in the same religious and cultural atmosphere as Pure Land and Nichiren Buddhism [an important Japanese sect focused on the teachings of the Lotus Sutra].

Zen cannot be divorced from its Indian and Chinese origins. As one Japanese scholar has described the subject, "Zen combined with the intellectual culture of India, the pragmatic culture of China, and the esthetic culture of Japan." The word *zen* derives from the Sanskrit word *dhyana*, meaning "meditation." However, the practice of meditation did not form the basis of a separate school until this stream had entered China, where it became related to Taoist conceptions and practices. The Chinese sects of Ch'an (Chinese for *dhyana*) formed the basis for the Japanese sects of Zen (the Japanese pronunciation of *Ch'an*). . . .

Dogen: Sitting in Meditation

Dogen (1200–53) [founder of the Soto School of Zen Buddhism] reportedly went to see Eisar [an important Zen teacher] after being disappointed in his own studies of Buddhism at Hieizan. After Eisai's death, Dogen traveled to China but could gain no satisfaction from the Buddhist teachings there. Finally he attained enlightenment under the guidance of a Chinese Zen master and received the training of the Ts'ao-tung sect. He returned to Japan to spread this new version of Zen. (*Ts'ao-tung* is pronounced *Soto* in Japanese.) However, Dogen was more uncompromising than Eisai and could not bring himself to serve the military rulers. This made his life difficult, but eventually his Soto sect of Zen flourished.

The difference between Rinzai Zen [taught by Eisai] and Soto Zen is roughly the same in China and Japan. Rinzai favors the use of techniques such as meditation on *koan* (which are comparable to riddles) to achieve sudden enlightenment. The Soto sect gives some weight to study of the scriptures and emphasizes the gradual entry into enlightenment. The Soto sect is famous for its practice of *zazen*, "sitting in meditation." Because of Dogen's two emphases "on scriptural authority and on faith in Buddha . . . the Soto Zen school in Japan was Dogen's unique creation." Within Japanese society, Rinzai came to be identified with the ruling class, Soto with the common people.

Dogen's system of thought is considered by Japanese scholars to be one of the most creative developments within Japanese Buddhism, and increasingly Western scholars have become attracted to Dogen's analysis of

A statue honoring the Buddha sits in Kyoto, Japan, where the spread of Buddhism is attributed to two sects that originated in China.

human existence and the nature of time. A distinctive feature of Zen teachings, both in China and in Japan, has been to emphasize a direct, intuitive transmission of the Buddha's enlightenment, and this is equally true for the transmission of Buddhist teaching about enlightenment from one master to his disciple. Dogen's meeting in China with the Chinese Zen (Ch'an) master Ju-ching was all-important in bringing Dogen to a realization of the direct, intuitive nature of enlightenment. According to tradition, Dogen was enlightened when he heard Ju-ching scolding a monk sleeping. Ju-ching said that instead of sleeping, the monk should "drop off the body and the mind." This brought home to Dogen the fact that true enlightenment meant leaving behind completely both mind and body. When Dogen set up his own monastic retreat, he emphasized loyalty to one's Zen master and meditation that went beyond thinking.

Dogen was critical of the Rinzai tradition of Zen Buddhism, which stressed meditation on *koan*. He feared that monks meditating on *koan* would become so engrossed in intellectual reflection on the *koan* that they would be deluded into thinking about enlightenment. For Dogen, the attaining of enlightenment was not a rational process or a solution to an intellectual puzzle. Enlightenment was more likely to be achieved by the total realization of the whole person than by intellectual activity. Instead of the *koan*, Dogen emphasized *zazen*. Although even sitting in meditation requires the use of the body and mind, Dogen stressed that the disciplining of body and mind in meditation facilitated the dropping off of body and mind. In other words, enlightenment is beyond matter and spirit. In fact, according to Dogen, one can enter enlightenment only after any thought of attaining enlightenment, or even any thought about enlightenment, has been eliminated. The way to free oneself from any such thoughts is just "to sit," to practice *zazen*. In a sense, one does not actually attain enlightenment, for there is no enlightenment to attain.

From the time Dogen first studied Buddhism at Hieizan, he had pondered the apparent contradiction of "original enlightenment" and "attained enlightenment." A person had to have some original potential for enlightenment or else one could not become enlightened. But if a person possessed the original enlightenment, then why did Buddhists find it so hard to strive to attain what they already possessed? Dogen's solution, reached through his own enlightenment experience, was that the contradiction appears because people think about enlightenment rather than practicing the way to enlightenment, *zazen*. A person who meditates in the proper fashion realizes that the practice of meditation and enlightenment are the same. In proper *zazen*, body and mind disappear automatically.

Dogen emphasized the importance of *zazen*, saying it superseded everything else. The experience of enlightenment within *zazen* reveals that the entire world is filled with the Buddha-nature. This is something that the unenlightened eye does not see but the enlightened eye is able to grasp immediately and intuitively.

Dogen stressed the primacy of *zazen* to the extent that he set forth a radical view of time. According to Dogen, only the moment of enlightenment has "reality," and both past and present are contained within the essence of this crucial moment. This did not mean that a person who attained enlightenment could stop practicing meditation. On the contrary, for Dogen believed that life is most important and most real when a person sits in meditation. His creative genius brought the discipline of meditation to a mature conclusion.

Zen: Institutional and Artistic Developments

Zen eventually assumed major importance in the Buddhist world. One landmark of Zen's success was the *shogun's* [political leader's] decree of 1338, "which led to the building of Zen temples in sixty-six localities." The temples, called *ankokuji*, or "temples to pacify the country," were similar in function to the earlier *kokubunji*, or provincial temples. Just as the *kokubunji* of the Nara period spread Buddhist teachings, so did the *ankokuji* of the fourteenth century help to spread Zen to the various regions of the country and to people of lower classes. The government recognized the top-ranking Zen temples (of the Rinzai sect), and the priests of these temples led the way in the study of Chinese classics and Neo-Confucianism.

Even Zen was no exception to the general tendency of Buddhist sects to undergo fluctuating periods of strength and weaknesses. For example, Dogen's thought and practice were very lofty, and he trained important disciples, but the development of Soto Zen into a major Buddhist denomination in Japan was mainly the work of Keizan (1268–1325), who lived shortly after the time of Dogen. Keizan was more willing than Dogen to compromise and blend with Zen other ritual practices. The simple funeral and memorial practices that he developed helped Soto Zen spread among the people much more thoroughly than Rinzai Zen. Later, the aristocratic Rinzai tended to lose its vigor, but in the eighteenth century, Hakuin (1686–1769) did much to revive Rinzai and meditation on *koan*. Hakuin is the author of the fa-

mous *koan* "Listen to the sound of the single hand"—
that is, to realize the sound of one hand clapping.

The seventeenth-century poet Basho (1644–94), who
also practiced Zen Buddhism, did much to further the
aesthetic expression of Zen in his beautiful short poems
called *haiku*. During Basho's last illness, while he was
on a trip, his followers asked him to give them a final
poem or "death poem." At first, Basho refused. But he
lived through the night, and the next morning he gave
them a poem based on his dreams during the night:

> On a journey, ill,
> and over fields all withered, dreams
> go wandering still.

Zen has its roots in India, emerged as a sect in China,
and first flourished in Japan as the imported Rinzai and
Soto sects. But Zen is much more than a sectarian expression of Buddhism or a personal experience of enlightenment. In both China and Japan, Zen had a
strong impact on the arts. Shingon had made some
contribution to the graphic arts; Zen pervaded the
whole culture. Zen (colored by Taoism's love of nature)
is the spiritual inspiration of much Chinese and Japanese painting; its influence can be seen in the art of
flower arranging (*ikebana*). Unlike Shingon art, which
favors the esoteric and borders on the grotesque, Zen
favors a quiet simplicity.

It is difficult to say whether the Chinese tradition of
Ch'an (Zen) taught quiet simplicity to the Japanese or
whether the Japanese brought a cultural tradition of
quiet simplicity to their understanding of Zen. However, from ancient times the Japanese have had a peculiar tradition combining aesthetic and religious appreciation of nature. This can be seen as early as the
eighth-century anthology of poetry, *Manyoshu*. Many

Westerners have come to appreciate Zen through translations of *haiku*, which express the spirit of Zen. Also, the drinking of tea and the cult of tea have been closely associated with Zen.

Zen has pervaded Japanese culture even beyond the realms of what Westerners ordinarily understand as art. Zen practitioners cared less for subtlety of doctrine than they cared for the complete training of mind and body. There was a relationship between emphasis on the instant of enlightenment and tuning the mind and body to every instant of experience. Therefore, military techniques or sports such as swordsmanship, archery, and wrestling were pursued for the sake of Zen. The object was not simply to defeat the opponent, but to tune one's whole being to a naturalness and freeness that transcended the formalities of prescribed movements. Kamakura warriors adopted Zen both for its utilitarian and its spiritual benefits. In the modern period, Zen continues to be a major inspiration for philosophical thought and religious cultivation.

A Young Woman Becomes a Zen Master

by Anonymous

The following selection is from a collection of Japanese Zen stories edited and translated by Thomas Cleary, whose other books include *The Five Houses of Zen* and *The Book of Serenity: 100 Zen Dialogues*. Concerned with the path to enlightenment of a young woman, the selection offers the paradoxes and surprises found in much of Zen literature, which are intended to serve as lessons. The young woman's example shows that meditation can take place anywhere, even while doing one's daily chores, as long as one's attention is focused. It also reflects Zen beliefs such as the ability to achieve flashes of enlightenment and that, ironically, some of the most enlightened souls are those who are troublesome and reject the teachings of experts. The selection also notes that once one understands the true nature of reality, that the world is transitory, and that all things are connected, there is no need to reject the world or, as the translator puts it, mundane reality. True Zen experts realize that we are never above the world but continue to live in it.

When Satsume was sixteen years old, she thought to herself, "Although I am not very beautiful, fortunately my body is sound. Undoubtedly I am to be married soon; I hope I get a handsome man."

Now she began to visit a certain shrine to pray, and she also started reciting a special scripture day and night. Even while she was doing her sewing and washing, the words of the scripture were constantly on her lips.

After several days of continual recitation, Satsume suddenly experienced an awakening of insight.

On one occasion, her father looked into her room and saw her sitting grandly on top of a copy of a Buddhist scripture. He was alarmed, thinking she may have gone mad; he gently admonished her, "What do you mean by sitting on a precious scripture? You will surely be punished by the Truth."

Satsume replied, "How is the wonderful scripture any different from my backside?"

Now her father thought this was even more bizarre; he went to tell the Zen master Hakuin.

Hakuin said, "I have a method that will help." He wrote a short poem, which he handed over and said, "Paste this on the wall of your home, where she will be sure to see it."

The poem said,

Hearing the call
of a silent raven
in the dark of night,
One misses one's father
before being born.

The man took the verse and did with it as Hakuin said. When she saw it, Satsume said, "This is the handwriting of master Hakuin. So even Hakuin only understands this much!"

Her father thought this was strange too, and told Hakuin about it. Hakuin said, "Bring Satsume here with you. I'll test her."

So Satsume and her father both came to visit Hakuin. The Zen master questioned the young woman closely, and Satsume answered fluently. Hakuin then presented a couple of koans [Zen riddles]. Satsume started thinking about them, but Hakuin said, "Go focus your mind on them."

Over a period of several days, Satsume passed through several levels of koans. Hakuin finally taught her that which goes beyond, but Satsume resisted and would not accept it. The Zen master then threw her out.

Satsume was ejected several times like this. By the time half a year had passed, she had seen through that which goes beyond and had thoroughly studied the most intricate and puzzling stories of the ancients. She was now a Zen master, even though still in her teens.

At this point, Satsume's father began looking for a suitable husband for her. At first she refused and would not marry, but Hakuin called her to him and said, "You have already seen through enlightened reality, so why should you reject mundane reality? What is more, marriage is an important duty for men and women. It would be better for you to go along with your father." So it was that Satsume got married.

After Satsume's passing, Hakuin's successor Suiwō said to his own disciples, "When our former teacher was alive, there were very many laywomen with perfectly clear insight. There were those among them like Old Lady Satsume, who were even beyond the reach of experienced Zen monks."

When Satsume was in her late years, she grieved exceptionally deeply over the loss of a granddaughter. The old man who lived next door chided her, "Why are you mourning so grievously? If people hear you, they'll wonder how you could still be acting like this even after having studied with Zen master Hakuin and attained insight into the essential. Please cut it down a little bit."

Satsume glared at the old man and retorted, "What do you know, baldy? My weeping and wailing are better for my granddaughter than incense, flowers, and lamps."

Zen in Daily Life: The Japanese Tea Ceremony

by William Theodore de Bary

Zen Buddhism in Japan was more than a form of religious faith. As the following selection asserts, it also had a major influence on Japanese culture as a whole, primarily during and after the Kamakura period (1192–1338). This selection focuses on the tea ceremony, a ritual related to the Japanese sense of repose and refinement that was also a reflection of many Zen beliefs. Zen masters crafted a tea ceremony in which the setting, the implements, the tea itself, and even the mode of drinking were intended to symbolize the transitional nature of earthly life and the possibility for the individual to both absorb a sense of his or her place in the flow of life and gain a hint of transcendence. The author of the selection is William Theodore de Bary, professor of east Asian studies at Columbia University.

The influence of Zen on Japanese culture was not limited to literature and art. There was a close connection between Zen and the Japanese warrior. Many samurai found Zen's stern masculinity and emphasis on intuitive action particularly congenial. For the believer in

Zen swordsmanship might even be considered "an art of protecting life" rather than a means of killing others, and during the Tokugawa period under Zen influence swordsmanship tended to become a peaceful art rather than a brutal contest.

The Importance of Tea

Perhaps, however, Zen's influence was nowhere more marked than in the evolution of the Japanese tea ceremony. The cult of tea was not exclusively affiliated with Zen Buddhism; during the Tokugawa shogunate [1600–1867] when [Chinese-style] Neo-Confucianism was the state philosophy, the tea ceremony came to be considered an effective means of training young women in the concept of *ri*, "ritual," here interpreted as the etiquette of the hearth. The tea cult also had its commercial aspects from the outset. Zen priests not only introduced the new beverage to Japan but also the pottery in which it was served, and the tea ceremony thus came to be not only a social attraction but a source of mercantile enterprise. These features of the background of the tea ceremony should not be ignored; nevertheless it remains true that it was the expression of many of the ideals of Buddhism, in particular of Zen Buddhism.

Three Zen masters were largely responsible for the growth of the tea cult in Japan. First was the founder of Japanese Zen, Eisai, who brought tea seeds home with him on his return from a second visit to China in 1191, and had them planted on a hillside near Kyoto. In 1214, as we have seen, he wrote the *Kissa yōjō-ki*, "Drink Tea To Nourish Life," in the hope of saving the Shogun [governor] Sanetomo from alcoholism by extolling the virtues of "the cup that cheers but does not inebriate."

In order to popularize the use of tea it was considered desirable to improve the quality of the cups in which it was served. Accordingly, when Dōgen [a monk who emphasized *zazen*, meditation] visited China in 1222 to study Zen, he was accompanied by an artisan who later established a thriving center of pottery production in Japan.

The next step was to create a setting for the demonstration of the methods of enjoying the new drink. It thus happened that when another Zen master, Musō Kokushi (1275–1351), had built a simple cottage in a secluded garden for the purpose of solitary meditation, it was found agreeable to have a nonintoxicating beverage as a mild stimulant. The three elements of the tea ceremony—the actual beverage, the pottery, and the setting—having thus been supplied, a cult before long developed with the active participation of Zen masters.

The tea hut was considered to consist of three elements—the exterior of the hut, the garden, and the interior. These were equated with three prime characteristics of Buddhist teaching: the evanescence of all things, the selflessness of all elements (dharmas), and the bliss of Nirvāna.

The Setting

Outside the cottage three things call one's attention to the first lesson in Buddhism, that life is everlasting change. The first is a little roof by the fence which, protecting the visitor from the weather, reminds him that nature is always changeable. This part is known as the *machiai*, or waiting house (a name which later acquired quite another meaning as a rendezvous for lovers). The second thing lies to the right in a thicket or under the shade of trees—a simple privy. Some may think that a privy hardly fits in with the exquisite refinement of the tea ceremony, but in fact it symbolizes better than anything else the incessant changes through which the human body passes. The third thing is the gate of the cottage, through which visitors constantly pass in and out, bending their heads and drawing up their legs as they do so, for the gate does not permit one to enter while standing upright.

The first lesson, the incessant changes of nature, is succeeded by the second one, in which three stone objects in the garden teach us the selflessness of the elements. These are the stepping stones, the stone water-basin, and the stone lantern, each silently teaching its lesson in selflessness. The flag-stones are willing to remain below and to be stepped on. The water-basin, where every visitor washes himself before entering the hut, may awaken the thought that the cleansing of the hands is made possible only by the willingness of the water to take away the dirt, the second example of selflessness. Lastly, there is a stone lantern which sheds a pale light. A little thought may lead to the realization of the selflessness of the wick, which is willing to be consumed in flame in order to illumine, however faintly, a dark corner of the garden.

The visitor is next led inside, into the room where the tea is to be served. After virtually doubling his body in order to pass through the low door, he suddenly finds himself in a realm of the most absolute peace. The room is small—only nine feet square and high—but everything in it is a marvel of purity and simplicity.

The first thing that greets the visitor is the scent of incense, which magically and indefinably transforms the atmosphere. Not only by its fragrance but by the faint wisp of its smoke does the incense catch the imagination. The ever-rising smoke symbolizes the constant aspiration of the terrestrial towards the celestial.

While the visitor sits motionlessly, watching in silence the course of the smoke, he is certain to hear the cries of a solitary bird flying by the hut, or the dripping of water in the fountain outside, or the rustle of the wind in the pines above the roof. Like the pealing of a distant temple bell, such sounds come from nowhere and lose themselves in timelessness, to awaken the enveloping silence from which all music comes and into which all music returns. Because these sounds are so fleeting, so transitory, the presence of silence is felt all the more profoundly. A moment has communion with eternity when sound meets silence to create music: this is the Buddhist philosophy of music expressed in the Avatamsaka doctrines [Indian Buddhist texts from about A.D. 300].

At the far end of the room, in the center, is an alcove in which hangs a scroll painting. Before it flowers are arranged. These two finite examples of form and color help to make visible the infinite, just as a single note can make us more aware of the eternal silence. Without forms of color the immense space surrounding us would remain forever a stupendous blank, an unnamable vacuum. When lines or colors cut through infinite space, painting, which is the meeting of the finite with the infinite, comes into being. The *Lotus Sūtra* [an important Buddhist text in China and Japan] says, "Everything finite tells of infinity."

Preparing the Tea

The appeal of the infinite having thus been made to the senses of smell, hearing, and sight, the visitor is now ready for the enjoyment of the tea. He will be mistaken, however, if he expects to witness anything extraordinary in the preparation. The host is seated by a small open fire with the paraphernalia required, including bamboo implements, lacquerware, pots, kettles, and silk napkins. There is not a single thing which the average Japanese family does not possess, for, as the Zen masters were accustomed to say, "Religion is a most ordinary thing." The teacups are somewhat larger than the usual ones and may be works of art, but they are made of nothing more extraordinary than clay; to the Zen believer the transformation of clay into a lovely teacup is religion itself.

In the actual preparation of the tea, the host must pay special attention to four things—the fire, the water, the spoon, and the bamboo whisk. The first two are powerful elements which in other circumstances require all of man's efforts to control; the second two, the spoon to measure the powdered tea and the whisk to stir it, require delicacy and care in order to ensure a perfect balance. When the host has placed the proper measure of tea in the cup, he pours in boiled water and stirs the mixture with the whisk until it is exactly right. Then it is placed before the visitor, who must lift the cup in both hands, feeling its texture and warmth. He drinks the tea, not in one gulp but three sips, savoring the liquid as refreshing as some precious elixir though made of a most common, ordinary leaf. Thus also is sometimes transformed the common clay of humanity into an arhant, [Buddhist saint] a bodhisattva [little Buddha], or a Buddha [enlightened one].

CHAPTER 4

Buddhism Around
the World and
in Modern Times

Religions and Religious Movements

Seeking the Bodhisattva Kuan Yin in Twentieth-Century China

by John Blofeld

The following selection is an account of British Buddhist John Blofeld's travels through China in the early twentieth century before the Communist takeover of that country in 1949. Blofeld focuses on stories, records, and accounts of Kuan Yin, the bodhisattva of compassion revered in Mahayana Buddhism. Bodhisattvas, key figures in Mahayana Buddhism, are enlightened souls, or Buddhas, who have put off entrance into nirvana so that they can make themselves available to help others seek enlightenment. Kuan Yin is a feminized derivation of Avalokiteshvara, one of the so-called celestial bodhisattvas of some of the pre-Mahayana schools of Buddhism that emerged in India in the last few centuries B.C. He was revered as a source of compassion and good fortune. Known as Kwannon in Japan, Kwanum in Korea, and Quan-an in Vietnam, Kuan Yin is an extremely popular figure. Although technically a bodhisattva, Mahayana Buddhists worship her as a "goddess" of love, forgiveness, and good luck. Even sailors give offerings to her to ensure their safety as they travel across seas and up rivers. Kuan Yin is frequently depicted in artwork, statuary, and even household knickknacks, and her image can be found in almost any east Asian gift shop.

In the following selection, Blofeld evinces the richness of Kuan Yin's presence and describes the ceremonies and poetry devoted to her. In so doing he provides a glimpse of how elements of Buddhist worship remained part of everyday life into modern times. John Blofeld is the author of many books concerned with China and its religions as well as *The Wheel of Life: The Autobiography of a Western Buddhist.*

During my early years in China, I once journeyed down the Cassia River [now the Lijiang River], having taken passage on a wooden vessel much larger than a sampan but not so large as to be properly called a junk. On the first part of the trip the sails were mostly furled, little canvas being needed to carry it through those swift waters, still less the great sweeps lying along the gunwales to either side. The powerful current had been a curse and was now a blessing to the crew (a grandfather, his two sons, their wives and several children) for, old and young, they had performed the up-river journey trudging doggedly along the slippery bank, bodies bent double as they hauled at the ropes harnessing them like draught-horses to their boat. Setting out from Kweilin [or Guilin, province in southern China] by moonlight, we awoke to find ourselves amidst the weird beauty of [Buddhist painter] Yang Su's grotesquely convoluted mountains, of which a Chinese proverb says: 'Though Kweilin's scenery is unequalled in this world, Yang Su's is even better', which may be taken to imply that Yang Su is part of heaven. If so, then heaven is a place very well worth visiting.

Among my fellow-passengers was a black-gowned, shaven-headed, wizened little person who looked so wise that one might easily suppose him a great Tripitaka [Buddhist scripture] Master rather than an ordinary monk. Inspired by this man's charm and the magic of those extraordinary surroundings, I spoke to him freely of the affinity that had drawn me to Kuan Yin, my doubts about the claims made in some of the texts recited in her honour and my being baffled by the varying accounts of her true nature. Having listened attentively, he replied:

'You think too much.' Then, holding up a lotus flower he had picked at dawn for his devotions, he exclaimed: 'Kuan Yin is here in front of your nose. Smell!'

Seeing the Bodhisattva Everywhere

Though he said no more on the subject, I recognised that one sentence as the most impressive sermon I had ever heard! That the freshness arising in the early morning from dew lying heavily upon the giant leaves carpeting a lotus pond is Kuan Yin's fragrance, or that the lotus—spotless purity arising from foetid mud—is preeminently her symbol, had not, I am sure, as much as entered his head. Quite simply he had told me that, in order to know her, I should yield my whole being to direct experience, to the sacred rites, for example, to the chanting of those passages I doubted, to the sonorous clang of bronze, the staccato throb of the wooden-fish drum, the golden candle-light playing upon her image and *whatever else might manifest itself* to a mind properly receptive; if allowed to work their magic unimpeded, these would best reveal the Bodhisattva's real nature.

His advice recurred to me through the years as opportunities for following it arose. Now and then, when left to my own devices in some house where I was a guest, I would be struck by a sudden intimation of Kuan Yin's presence and know without looking that, behind a screen or in some recess or corner partly concealed from the rest of the room, stood a shrine to her. Perhaps it would prove to be a trifling affair—just a footwide altar-shelf or a glass and blackwood cabinet no larger than a fair-sized tea caddy containing a small statue of her in snowy porcelain, a miniature incense-burner, a pair of tiny candlesticks and a couple of little flower-vases to match, flowers and a few pretty trifles reminiscent of the sea such as ornaments of pearl or coral. Even if smoke were still arising from an incense stick lit for morning or evening devotions, I would know that that was not the reason for my apprehension of her presence, since house-shrines may contain a likeness of any one of China's innumerable deities and yet arouse no sense of a brooding presence.

At times the experience would be so powerful that, had she suddenly materialised, I would have deemed that almost less miraculous than the fact of her actually being there and yet not palpable to my senses. This occurred more than once during my visits to places known as 'halls of virtue'—a great feature of South China. Serving occasionally as homes for the aged, but more often as dwellings for communities of men or women living in semi-retirement from the world, they were to be found in the suburbs of many cities, as they are to this day in those parts of Southeast Asia with large Chinese communities. One comes upon an ornamental gateway giving access to some pleasant spot where upward-sweeping roofs peep from among a grove of trees. They are in fact small temples backed by courtyards with dormitories or rows of cell-like rooms occupied by recluses who may be dressed in sober monastic gowns. One's sense of Kuan Yin's actual presence has nothing to do with the appearance of her shrine or the architectural features of the surroundings, because very similar places may give one the feeling that she is not and has never been there; she is drawn, I think, by the purity of the inmates, their unassuming simplicity, their endeavours to live compassionately thinking no harm to the smallest insect let alone eating animal flesh, and the gentleness of their ways to one another and all about them. One has but to look into their eyes to know the fruits of devotion to Kuan Yin.

Devotion to Kuan Yin in Japan

This attitude of joyous devotion is also prevalent in Japan, where Kuan Yin Bodhisattva goes by the name of Kwannon-sama. My favourite memories of a recent visit to that country are of bands of pilgrims plodding on foot from one holy place to another in a pleasantly wooded, mountainous region. Their white pilgrim surcoats gleamed like patches of snow against the sombre green of giant pines and cedars towering above a grey expanse of massive curving roofs. In those solitary places, except for the cries of birds or the soothing sound of water tumbling down a slope, a marvellous stillness reigns—a stillness made all the more impressive by contrast with the occasional boom of an age-green temple bell of vast proportions. But with the pilgrims comes a sudden spate of cheerful noise—shuffling foot-falls, the thud of pilgrim staves upon the rugged path, the tinkle of the bells they carry suspended from their garments and the laughing chatter of simple folk who feel perfectly assured that every step of the way brings them nearer to rebirth in Amida (Amitābha)'s or Kwannon-sama's Pure Land. The joyful serenity of their faith is often expressed in tiny fragments of song known as *waka*, which are longer than *haiku* [three-line poems often used in Zen Buddhist worship] but just as rich in delicate allusions. These include some songs in honour of Kwannon-sama, of which the appropriate one is sung on arrival at each of thirty-three temples containing notable images of that Bodhisattva. For example:

'The spirit wishing for the next life may be light. Not so the Buddha's pledge, firm as a rocky mountain.'

or

'Having left our native place and come at last to this Kimiyedera temple, how close are we now to the Capital!' [*wherein the last word, though seemingly signifying Kyoto, means in fact the Pure Land to which Kwannon-sama will surely lead them*]

Another of these little songs implies that Kwannon-sama, by graciously transforming ordinary appearances, provides pilgrims with a foretaste of the beauty of her Pure Land. It runs:

'Looking again this morning, I realised it was but morning dew upon the moss in this Oka-dera temple garden—it was just like shining crystal!'

Yet another, addressed to Jundei—one of the many-armed forms of Kwannon-sama—stresses absolute conviction of the reliability of her vow to deliver all beings, no matter what their failings:

'However great our load of evil karma, it surely can be remedied by prayer—so firm this Jundei Hall!'

I am sure Japan contains many erudite Buddhists

who share the more subtle Chinese interpretations of Kuan Yin's nature, but I know too little of them to be able to adduce as many comparisons with the Bodhisattva's devotees in China as I could wish.

To witness a full-scale performance of Kuan Yin's rites, it is best to visit a large temple, whether in China or Japan or one of the neighbouring countries, during any of three great annual festivals which fall respectively on the nineteenth day of the second, sixth and ninth lunar months. First comes her 'birthday' (a surprising term when one reflects that she is not a historical personage but born of a ray of light issuing from Amitābha Buddha's [the Buddha associated with Pure Land Buddhism] eye); next comes the feast celebrating her vow to renounce Nirvāna's final peace while any beings still wander in samsara's [the cycle of death and rebirth] round; and then follows the feast celebrating her assumption of Bodhisattvahood. Once I was fortunate enough to witness such a festival at a large temple on the seacoast in the vicinity of Amoy, a place with the usual lovely Chinese roofs but notable for walls built of red brick instead of grey. Cleanliness being considered an essential counterpart of inner purity, the Hall of the Three Buddhas and the special shrine to Kuan Yin had received such a sweeping and a scouring that not a speck of dust was to be found there. Moreover, the nuns and lay-recluses who had come in from round about to join the monks in celebrating the festival had made a point of taking a ritual bath—but whether or not in the sea, I do not remember.

A Rite for Kuan Yin

When the time came for the great evening rite, candles blazed, clouds of perfumed smoke rose from a dozen censers disposed throughout the public parts of the temple, and the altars were decked with a rich profusion of fruit and flowers. Those taking part belonged to four separate communities—monks with jade-clasped *kasa* (togas) of brown silk or fine cloth worn over full-sleeved gowns of black cotton in a fashion that recalled the yellow robes worn by Buddhist monks in tropical countries; nuns, also shaven-headed and in black robes but with discernible hints of gleaming white under-jackets at throat and sleeves, an unwonted smartness appropriate to the occasion; female recluses in ceremonial robes of plain white; and ordinary people like myself, dressed for the most part in traditional Chinese silken gowns, but not without a sprinkling of men in Western-style suits. All but this last group had certainly purified themselves not merely by ablutions, but also by a period of silent contemplation to banish worldly thoughts and every other kind of thought extraneous to the rites. The appearance of the whole assembly was clean and richly sombre, there being no ostentation of any kind.

Summoned by the thunder of a giant drum, the devotees went to their appointed places, monks on the right of the assembly with the ordinary laymen behind them, nuns on the left backed by the white-gowned recluses. Each, on reaching his kneeling cushion, fell thrice to his knees touching head to the ground; and, when a signal rang out from the bronze sounding-bowl, this triple obeisance was repeated in unison. Though at least two hundred people took part and the obeisance is a complicated one, their movements were beautifully synchronised to accord with signals made by several kinds of metal percussion instrument. So in days gone by had the mandarins prostrated themselves before the Son of

Heaven at the dawn levee in the Forbidden City [the emperor's palace in Beijing, China's capital].

Now a sweet and lingering note was struck; to the throb of an enormous wooden-fish drum the incense paeon arose, a solemn succession of long-drawn cadences more varied than a chant and yet not quite a song. Addressed not to Kuan Yin but to the Dharma Lord (the Buddha), it placed the rites in their proper perspective; for, to her Buddhist followers at least, Kuan Yin is not the central deity of a separate cult and her worship conforms in all respects with the teaching and practice of Mahayana Buddhism.

> Excellent fragrance,
> Glowing in the precious tripod,
> Permeates the universe,
> An offering to the Dharma Lord.
> May he blessedly endure
> For as long as sky and earth shall last!
> May he blessedly endure
> For as long as sky and earth shall last!
>
> Hail to the Bodhisattvas
> Borne upon these perfumed clouds!
>
> The effulgence of holiness and virtue
> May be likened to these spreading clouds.
> The Bodhi-Mind, immeasurably vast,
> Spreads forth its shining filaments.
> We pay reverence to the Dharma Lord,
> Praying that all may be auspicious.
> Hail to the Bodhisattvas
> Within this canopy of perfumed clouds!

A Westerner Explains His Attraction to Zen Buddhism

by Alan Watts

Zen Buddhism began to grow popular in the United States in the 1950s and 1960s, especially among disaffected young people seeking alternatives to what they saw as the emptiness and conformity of modern life. Alan Watts, the author of the following selection, was one of the leading figures in popularizing Zen in America. Born in England, Watts received a master's degree from Seabury-Western Theological Seminary in Illinois and was an ordained Episcopalian minister who taught at Harvard University. During the latter years of his life he lived in the San Francisco Bay area, where he frequently gave lectures and held seminars on the appeal of Zen. Watts died in 1973, but in the months prior to his death he gave a number of talks aboard his Sausalito, California–based houseboat. The selection is taken from the tapes of those talks. In it, he explains why he finds Zen Buddhism appealing and suggests certain ways it is a compelling challenge to westerners.

Why study Zen? The first reason that occurs to me is that it is extremely interesting. Since childhood I have been fascinated by the mystery of being, and it has always struck me as absolutely marvelous that this universe in which we live is here at all. And just out of sheer wonder I have become interested in all of the various answers that people have given as to why all of this is here.

In this sense my approach to religion is not so much that of the moralist as of the scientist. A physicist may have a well-developed and highly concrete experimental approach to nature, but a good physicist is not necessarily an improved man or woman in the sense of being morally superior. Physicists know certain things, and their knowledge is power, but that does not automatically improve them as people. And the power they have may be used for good or for evil.

But indeed, they do have power, and they have gained that power through their knowledge. I have always thought that in many ways Zen is like Western science; Zen has been used for healing people's sicknesses, but it has also been used by the samurai for chopping off people's heads!

The Sameness of Spiritual Experience

I am interested in Zen for what it reveals about the way the universe is, the way nature is, and what this world is doing. My interest is part and parcel of a greater inquiry, which boils down to this: If you read the literature of the great religions, time and time again you come across descriptions of what is usually referred to as "spiritual experience." You will find that in all the various traditions this modality of spiritual experience seems to be the same, whether it occurs in the Christian West, the Islamic Middle East, the Hindu world of Asia, or the Buddhist world. In each culture, it is quite definitely the same experience, and it is characterized by the transcendence of individuality and by a sensation of being one with the total energy of the universe.

This experience has always fascinated me, and I have been interested in the psychological dynamics of it: why it happens, what happens, and how it comes to be described in different symbols with different languages. I wanted to see if I could discover the means of bringing this kind of experience about, because I have often felt that the traditional ways of cultivating it are analogous perhaps to medieval medicine. There a concoction is prepared consisting of roasted toads, rope from the gallows, henbane, mandrake, a boiled red dog, and all manner of such things, and a great brew is made! I assume that someone in the old folk tradition from which these recipes came understood the potencies of the brew, and that this thing really did do some good. But a modern biochemist would take a look at that mixture and say, "Well, it may have done some good, but what was the essential ingredient?"

In the same way, I ask this question when people sit in Zen meditation, practice yoga, or practice the [Hindu] bhakti way of religious devotion. What is the essential ingredient? In fact I ask this question of all the various things people do, even when they take psychedelic chemicals. No matter what methods people choose, it is interesting to look at what element these methods share in common. If we eliminate the nonsense and the nostalgia that go with people's attachment to a particular cultural approach, what is left?

The Essential Spiritual Experience

It has always struck me as a student of these things that Zen has come very close to the essentials. At least this was my first impression, partly because of the way D.T. Suzuki [a Japanese monk who helped introduce Zen Buddhism to the West in the early 20th century] presented Zen. It seemed to me to be the "direct way," the sudden way of seeing right through into one's nature—*right now*, at this moment. There is a good deal of talk about that realization in Zen circles, and in some ways it is more talk than practice. I remember a dinner once with [Sabro] Hasegawa [a San Francisco–based Zen artist], when somebody asked him, "How long does it take to obtain our understanding of Zen?"

He said, "It may take you three minutes; it may take you thirty years. And," he said, "I mean that."

It is that *three minutes* that tantalizes people! We in the West want instant results, and one of the difficulties of instant results is that they are sometimes of poor quality. I often describe instant coffee as a punishment for people who are in too much of a hurry to make real coffee! There is something to be said against being in a hurry.

There are two sides to this question, and it strikes me in this way: It's not a matter of time at all. The people who think it ought to take a long time are of one school of thought, and the people who want it quickly are of another, and they are both wrong. The transformation of consciousness is not a question of how much time you put into it, as if it were all added up on some sort of quantitative scale, and you got rewarded according to the amount of effort you put into it. Nor is there a way of avoiding the effort just because you happen to be lazy, or because you say, "I want it now!"

The point is, rather, something like this: If you try to get it either by an instant method because you are lazy or by a long-term method because you are rigorous, you'll discover that you can't get it *either* way. The only thing that your effort—or absence of effort—can teach you is that your effort doesn't work.

The answer is found in the middle way—and Buddhism is called the Middle Way—but it is not just some sort of compromise. Instead, "middle" here means instead "above and beyond extremes."

A Biblical Comparison

It is put this way in the Bible: "To him that hath shall be given." Or, to put it another way, you can *only* get it when you discover that you don't need it. You can only get it when you *don't* want it. And so instead you ask, "How do I learn *not* to want it, *not* to go after it, either by the long-term method or by the instant method?" But obviously if you ask that, you still are seeking it, and thereby not getting it!

A Zen master says, "If you have a stick, I will give you one. If you have not, I will take it away from you." Of course this is the same idea as "to him that hath shall be given; and from him that hath not, shall be taken away even that which he hath." So we find ourselves in a situation where it seems that all our normal thinking—all the ways we are accustomed to thinking about solving problems—doesn't work. All thinking based on acquisition is rendered obsolete. We have, as it were, to get into a new dimension altogether to approach this question.

A young Zen student I know said to me recently, "If I were asked what is really essential in Zen, it would be *sanzen*." Sanzen is the dialogue between the master and the student, the person-to-person contact. He said rather than *zazen*, or sitting meditation, it is *sanzen* that is the crux of it. It is in the peculiar circumstances of that dialog that we can get into the frame of mind I am talking about.

In effect this dialog acts as a mirror to one's own mind, because the teacher always throws back to the student the question he's asked! He really does not answer any questions at all, he merely tosses them back at you, so that you yourself will ask *why* you are asking it, and why you are creating the problem the question expresses.

And quickly it becomes apparent that it is up to you. "Who, *me?*" you may ask. *Yes, you!* "Well," you may say, "I can't solve this problem. I don't know how to do it."

But what do you mean by *you?* Who are you, really? Show me the you that cannot answer the question. It is in this kind of back-and-forth dialogue that you begin to understand. Through relationship with the other person you discover that it is you who's mixed up, and that you are asking the wrong questions! In fact, you are trying to solve the wrong problem altogether.

An Activist Monk from War-Torn Vietnam

by John Prados

Vietnamese Buddhism is mainly of the Mahayana variety, adapted from the practices of Vietnam's large neighbor to the north, China. But beyond its Mahayana roots, Buddhism in Vietnam has been the product of the nation's unique history and experiences. Many Buddhists in southern Vietnam, for instance, cling to Theravada Buddhism because of that region's long connection to Cambodia. Even many Mahayana monks around the country continue to wear the saffron-colored robes associated with Theravada monasteries. Outside the monasteries ordinary people often combine Buddhist practices with Confucianism and ancestor worship from China or spirit worship from Cambodia or Laos.

In the following selection, historian John Prados describes a Vietnamese monk who was forced to respond to the circumstances of his era: the Vietnam War, which lasted from 1946 to 1975 (the American phase of the war was from 1956 to 1975). In these years, during most of which Vietnam was divided and badly governed, monks such as Thich Nhat Hanh became active social reformers. They sought both to defend themselves and their orders from government threats and to bring

John Prados, *The Hidden History of the Vietnam War*. Chicago, IL: Ivan R. Dee, 1995. Copyright © 1995 by John Prados. Reproduced by permission of the publisher.

peace and understanding to their troubled people. Rather than retreat to a monastery, Prados notes, Hanh started schools and other institutions and lobbied government officials, and he remained an activist even after the war was over. He was part of a larger movement of Buddhist protest during the war years, which sometimes, as in the famous 1963 case of Thich Quang Duc, involved members' burning themselves to death publicly as a form of nonviolent resistance.

John Prados is the author of many books on military history, including *The Soviet Estimate: U.S. Intelligence and Soviet Strategic Forces* and *Presidents' Secret Wars: CIA and Pentagon Covert Operations from World War II to Iranscam.*

One Buddhist thinker whose life well illustrates the sad effects of the Vietnam War is Thich Nhat Hanh. Among those bonzes [monks] who responded to the calls for an "engaged Buddhism" that assisted social reform, Hanh became a key theoretician and is known today as the exponent of the philosophy of "Mindfulness" and founder of the Interbeing movement. Nhat Hanh's repeated tours of the United States and Europe, and the Buddhist communities he has established in France, have had an impact on religious practice in the West as well as some effect in supporting continued efforts of Vietnamese Buddhists to achieve free practice of their religion in socialist Vietnam. Along the way, Thich Nhat Hanh's stormy life stands as an example of just how difficult has been the path of Buddhism in Vietnam.

Born in the central area of Vietnam in 1926, he began early to study Buddhist texts and was ordained a monk at age sixteen at the height of World War II. Be-

coming Thich Nhat Hanh, he wrote poetry and sermons (Buddhists call them "dharma talks") that were
among the most popular presented by bonzes of his
generation. Hanh was among the founders of the An
Quang pagoda in 1950 and subscribed to "engaged
Buddhism" even before the time of Ngo Dinh Diem
[president of Vietnam, 1954–1963]. When An Quang
became the Buddhist Institute, Hanh was one of its first
professors, having lectured at the pagoda since 1954. It
is a measure of antagonisms between traditional and
engaged Buddhism that lay authorities at both the An
Quang and Xa Loi pagodas struck Hanh's name from
the *livrets de famille* [family histories] of those temples,
in effect preventing Hanh from presenting courses or
residing at them.

Thich Nhat Hanh first traveled to the United States
in 1961; he studied comparative religion at Princeton
and taught at Columbia University. In New York at the
time of Diem's demise [November 1963], Hanh was
torn by the urge to return to his native country, but he
felt put off by the lack of support for his earlier reform
efforts, especially a lack of support from Thich Tri
Quang. Columbia asked Hanh to stay and offered to
create a department of Vietnamese studies around him.
But Hanh received a letter from Tri Quang, who said he
had grown too old and old-fashioned to be the intellectual leader of the new Buddhist movement (though
he was just three years older than Hanh). Hanh returned to Vietnam, where he became a principal drafter
of the program of the Unified Buddhist Church
adopted by a national religious conference in January
1964, as well as a prime mover in forming the Vanh
Hanh University and the School of Youth for Social Service, whose first head was one of Hanh's former stu-

dents. Thich Nhat Hanh himself became the first director of social studies at Vanh Hanh University.

Resuming his social activism, in early 1964 Hanh began leading teams of disciples, activists, and experts to remote villages damaged by the war. During one such mission, after devastating floods at the New Year of 1965, Hanh's team had to thread its way carefully between South Vietnamese troops and Viet Cong [South Vietnamese Communist insurgents] fighting in the area. The bonze's protégés continued this work, helping villages build schools and health clinics, and even setting up pilot villages. Some Schools of Youth for Social Service adherents died in various incidents, including at least one grenade attack on the school itself. The work continued despite later action by the Vanh Hanh University severing its affiliation with the school. By 1975 some ten thousand persons were involved in the social work, and the school had been written up in the American press as a "little" Peace Corps.

Thich Nhat Hanh also continued his writing and became chief editor of the La Boi Press, a Buddhist publishing house, as well as editor of the official publication of the Unified Buddhist Church. In February 1966 he founded a religious order, Tiep Hien, formally consecrating his philosophy of Interbeing. Later that year he was invited to undertake a lecture tour of the United States by the Fellowship for Reconciliation and Cornell University. Advocating negotiations and "peace"—which by this time South Vietnamese government circles regarded as Communist provocation—brought an edict against Hanh's return to Vietnam, a ban continued by the subsequent Communist government of unified Vietnam. Thich Nhat Hanh has lived in exile ever since.

From Hanh's point of view, peace was necessary to

stop the suffering of the Vietnamese people, and he continued to press these views throughout the remainder of the war. His best-known political work, *Vietnam: Lotus in a Sea of Fire*, was published in the United States in 1967. He also pressed his views in meetings with Secretary of Defense [Robert] McNamara, in audiences with Pope Paul VI, and on lecture trips in Europe and the United States. Assisted by Chan Khong, a dedicated nun of his Tiep Hien order, Hanh formed a Buddhist peace delegation in Paris to press for an end to the war during the period of the Paris negotiations from 1969 to 1973. Throughout this period they collected donations and furnished support for Buddhist social activists still engaged in Vietnam. Hanh also met with American political figures, including Robert F. Kennedy and Senator J. William Fulbright, and in 1967 he was nominated for the Nobel Peace Prize by Martin Luther King, Jr.

Since the war Hanh has founded a Buddhist collective, called Plum Village, near Bordeaux, France, and has continued his efforts in behalf of Buddhists in Vietnam while focusing on more general religious teaching. In 1976 and 1977 Hanh and Chan Khong sailed in the Gulf of Siam, helping in the rescue of the Vietnamese boat people. The two have made appeals to the current Vietnamese government in favor of Buddhists and freedom of religion, and Chan Khong continues to raise money for social and religious projects in Vietnam.

At last count Thich Nhat Hanh had published more than ninety books and pamphlets, mostly on religious themes and in Vietnamese. The bonze continues to tour and to present dharma talks to interested audiences, including more than seven tours of the United States since the early 1980s. Where a dharma talk at Berkeley, California, in 1985 drew an audience of four hundred, in 1990 avid listeners in the same city packed a four-thousand-seat auditorium. That year Hanh held a special retreat only for Vietnam veterans, and he came away appreciating their particular problems in working through their Vietnam experiences. "The veterans have something to tell their nation about how to deal with problems that are likely to happen," Hanh later wrote, "problems that will not look different from Vietnam."

An Isolated Buddhist Kingdom Faces the Modern World

by Barbara Crossette

The following selection concerns the fate of Bhutan, a tiny nation high in the Himalaya Mountains between India and China. Bhutan was one of a number of mountain kingdoms that around one thousand years ago, adopted the so-called tantric form of Buddhism. Tantric Buddhism, a branch of the Mahayana school, was partially adapted from the tantra practiced in Hinduism, which suggested that esoteric rituals and magic were an important part of spiritual realization. For Buddhists, tantrism requires close training with a lama, or teacher, who serves as a guide to the understanding of the ultimate reality, of the oneness of all things and experiences.

To modern westerners the best known of these Himalayan tantric kingdoms is Tibet, which in the 1950s was conquered and then incorporated into Communist China. Other kingdoms include Ladakh and Sikkim, now part of India, and Nepal, where the locals practice a mixture of Hinduism and Buddhism. Only Bhutan remains independent and Buddhist, but as Barbara Crossette, the author of the selection, claims, the nation is challenged from both outside and inside by tourism, in-

Barbara Crossette, *So Close to Heaven: The Vanishing Buddhist Kingdoms of the Himalayas*. New York: Alfred A. Knopf, 1995. Copyright © 1995 by Barbara Crossette. All rights reserved. Reproduced by permission of Alfred A. Knopf, Inc., a division of Random House, Inc.

ward migration, and the influence of popular culture. Such challenges, she writes, have sometimes led even the Bhutanese to desecrate temples and commit even worse crimes. Barbara Crossette was a *New York Times* correspondent in Asia for seven years and has taught journalism at universities in India and the United States.

I am haunted by a particular front page of *Kuensel*, Bhutan's only newspaper. *Kuensel* is a weekly publication, and the date of this issue is April 10, 1993. The page is dominated by a large photograph of five young men in disheveled versions of the robelike garment, the *gho*, that Bhutanese men have worn for centuries. The shifty-eyed youth on the far right, on the edge of what is obviously an identity parade arranged by the police, looks uneasy and seems to be leaning out of this grisly group portrait. The one on the left appears slightly deformed or otherwise handicapped and has a hunted look. The three in the middle are fresh-faced, clean-cut lads who stare straight ahead, with little expression. In Bhutan, the last independent Himalayan Buddhist kingdom, a mountain paradise that only yesterday seemed untarnished by brutality or greed, the crime that this band of rural ruffians stands accused of is beyond atrocity: slitting the throat of an elderly monk (who had just given them food and a place to sleep) and smashing with a hammer and ax the heads of his two novices, in the hope of making off with a few treasures from the holy man's temple.

But that isn't all of the story. The gang failed to accomplish their goal of snatching the relics from Chimme Lhakhang, an isolated shrine, because they were interrupted by the screams of a village woman somewhere down the hill, and they fled. She was shouting, "Someone is being killed!" Unknown to the murderers in the temple, however, she wasn't exposing them. She was alerting her neighbors to her own situation. In a land where the avoidance of violence is a cultural assumption and women are strong, her husband was beating her to death.

The imagery is jarring. Isn't this supposed to be a Buddhist kingdom dedicated to the ideals of a nonviolent religion that sometimes seems more like an ethical system than a creed? Didn't I come here to see Buddhism as it is lived from day to day in a country that is the last of its line? Everywhere else in the Himalayan Buddhist world, people talked about how things used to be. Go to Bhutan, they said, where the universe is intact.

For decades, many Westerners repelled by materialism and a surfeit of industrial development have sought solace and reassurance in the Buddhist and Hindu East. In recent years, especially in India and Nepal, such sojourns have involved a certain measure of denial. Like writers looking for only those facts or quotes that will back a preconceived conclusion, spiritual tourists and other romantics who roam the Indian subcontinent and the Himalayas often bypass the worldly horrors around them: too many people, too little food, scant respect for nature, and a dearth of humane national policies to match professed beliefs and moral postures. To experience close-up the Eastern transcendence they extol from afar, outsiders must not look too closely at the commercialization of spirituality either—at the temple touts, the gold-plated gurus, the factory-wrapped loaves of sliced white bread left as offerings to the gods.

A Unique Kingdom

Denial, however, has never been demanded of visitors to Bhutan. In the increasingly choked and often turbulent regions of inner Asia, Bhutan—the nation known to its Buddhist majority as Druk Yul, the Kingdom of the Thunder Dragon—stood alone as a nation unsullied. It was a place where, despite a punishing terrain, life was (and mostly still is) lived at a different pace and with attractive values, among them a strong sense of individual self-reliance within supportive communities, an openness of spirit, and a large measure of self-respect that makes people look foreigners in the eye as equals. Bhutanese live in sturdy houses of mud walls and wooden half-timbering below gently pitched roofs finished with rough shingles held down by rocks. Woodwork and sometimes outer walls are decorated by village craftsmen in gently muted colors with designs drawn from Buddhist iconography and folklore. There are towns—I think of Mongar, Tongsa, or Tashigang—where clusters of painted, ornamented buildings could have materialized from illustrations in old fairy tales.

The land the Bhutanese inhabit, wedged between the world's two most populous countries, China and India, could also be drawn from the pages of a storybook. Spread over soaring icy mountains, black-dark gorges echoing with the roar of rushing water, emerald valleys silent under the sun, and forests rustling day and night with life of every kind, Bhutan is the size of Switzerland but has fewer than a million people, no cities as we know them, and no more than half a dozen paved roads of any significance. More people walk or travel by horseback than ride in motorized vehicles of any kind; topography ensures that this transportation pattern will endure indefinitely. The leg muscles of the

Bhutanese, men and women, are magnificent. It takes strength and energy to live, as most Bhutanese do, at altitudes above five thousand feet, sometimes in villages so impossibly high above the valleys they farm that a lowlander can only stand and stare in disbelief at the precipitous passage between the warmth of home and the necessities and temptations provided by the outside world. And then urban life may be represented by no more than a ramshackle market stall at the side of the nearest (a relative term here) road. For the Bhutanese man or woman who leaves such an environment for a trip abroad, international travel is the easy part, or so Ugyen Dorji of the Jichu Drake Bakery told me with astonishing matter-of-factness as he described how he, a village boy, was shipped to Austria to be trained in pastrymaking under one of the more unusual national human resources policies. For him, the Austrian Alps were hardly worth writing home about.

Bhutan has had a modern capital (though mostly housed in a walled fortress) for less than half a century. In the rankings of world capitals, Thimphu has few competitors among the miniatures. Had it not just got its first traffic light, Thimphu and its mere hundreds of homes and wood-fronted shops arranged along a few short paved roads—only one of them connecting the town to anywhere else in the country—might have survived into the twenty-first century as the most bucolic seat of government on earth. With no airport or train station disgorging newcomers (just flocks of small buses, which, wisely, don't ply the narrow mountain roads at night), Thimphu has not had much of an opportunity to develop the ubiquitous landmarks that make so many cities interchangeable, forcing the traveler to get out of town in order to see the country. Although it may not seem so to Bhutanese from the distant hills, Thimphu (with something like twenty thousand people; no one seems sure) *is* Bhutan from the moment of arrival. Mountains enclose it, monasteries and temples define its skyline, national building codes require that its homes and shops (there are no industries) hew to traditional architectural styles, strolling monks and farmers people its few pavements and numerous earthen byways, mingling with the modernized hustlers of a burgeoning middle class and the knots of idle young men caught somewhere between a subsistence past and a money economy.

At about seven thousand feet altitude, Thimphu and its environs along a willow-lined river are also much like the other high mountain valleys in which the majority of Bhutanese, and many other Himalayan people, live. Bhutan has four major climatological and topographical bands, but most of its towns and villages grew up historically in temperate regions stretching from east to west along the country's mountainous but fertile midsection from Thimphu to Tashigang. To the south of this strip there are a band of cooler broadleaf forests and then a subtropical zone. To the north there is alpine scrub, and the snow line that announces the high Himalayan peaks stretching along the frontier with Tibet.

Until relatively recently, Bhutanese Buddhists from the temperate valleys had no interest in the steamy southern lands along the Indian border, where the vegetation is subtropical and rain is heavy during monsoons, though there are no true rain forests. Heat, disease, pests, and soil inhospitable to the grain crops and vegetables preferred by many Bhutanese made the south unattractive. Spurning the south, however, meant leaving it open to influxes of immigrants, most of them Hindus from Nepal and India. Political and ethnic tensions followed. . . .

Stealing from Temples

For many years before and after [eighteenth-century British explorers Samuel] Bogle and [George] Davis, the Bhutanese, guided by a policy of wariness and aided by geography, shut out the world almost entirely. In the latter part of the twentieth century, as other once-closed Himalayan realms—Nepal, Ladakh, Sikkim, and Tibet—were opening to tourism, Bhutan held back, fearful of scarring its unspoiled terrain and turning its spontaneous, pervasive religiosity into a Buddhist performance for camcorders. When tourists finally began to arrive, limits were placed on their numbers.

But the Bhutanese are discovering that tourism may not be their most pressing problem. Some disturbing changes that threaten this unique Himalayan culture are springing from within the Bhutanese themselves as they proceed, through trial and error, toward integration into the wider world. What Bhutan is going through now should be of interest to all of us who worry about how an overcrowded planet increasingly headed toward a crisis of physical survival in the next century, especially in South Asia, will cope with the primal screams of small, endangered human cultures that get in the way of the scramble for farmland and living space.

But even among these threatened communities, the Bhutanese stand apart. Many of Asia's endangered societies are tribal—food-gatherers or pastoral nomads whose development stopped at a basic level of subsistence—and they attract the sympathy and support of anthropologists and good-hearted laypeople, particularly in Europe, who form paternalistic committees and organize demonstrations to look after their interests. The Bhutanese—proud, capable, lonely survivors of a developed ancient civilization of scholastic brilliance and considerable social achievement—are far removed in time and lifestyle from tribalism, by any definition. No charitable crusaders panting to save the world's naïfs reach out to them; in any case, they would disdain that kind of help. The few foreigners allowed to live in the Dragon Kingdom, ostensibly to help develop it, soon learn that the Bhutanese always do things their own way and in their own time. Down to the lowest farmer, they need to be convinced that something new being dangled before them is something they need and want. Then there's no stopping them.

In an electronic age, and at a time when people can move from place to place with relative ease, defying almost any nation's efforts to close its borders, the world beyond Bhutan intrudes with or without the catalyst of tourists or other visiting foreigners. The Bhutanese king's periodic orders banning satellite dishes become gestures sadly close to commanding the sea to hold back, because television receivers *are* permitted, and they connect to video players, bringing tales of casual violence to people barely out of an age of mythology. The five young men accused of killing the lama of Chimme Lhakhang and his two novices apparently told the police that they identified with the high-living gangsters they saw in cheap video films flooding the country from India, Hong Kong, and Bangkok. Or at least that's the way the police wanted the story to be told. "The motive for the murder was not village vendetta, revenge, or reprisal, but purely greed," the police told *Kuensel.* "Such cold-blooded murders are normally unheard of in this country."

If murder is still rare, theft from religious monuments is not, and this may sooner or later lead to the locking away of more temple treasures. Because icons and chortens, or shrines, are known to contain objects of value—if not pure silver and gold, certainly semi-precious stones—they are increasingly the targets of thieves no longer fearful of divine retribution for tampering with holy relics. Among the stones are corals, turquoise, and agates called *zi*, which many Himalayan Buddhists believe have been put in place by the gods themselves. *Zi* are small stones etched with white stripes in a process that has apparently been lost over the centuries, thus giving rise to the legend that the stones had miraculous origins. These old stones command very high prices from collectors. King Jigme Singye Wangchuck says that because of the lucrative market for relics from the last Himalayan Buddhist kingdom, there are hardly any chortens in Bhutan that have not been pilfered. Those in lonely spots along near-empty roads or on hilltops are most vulnerable; some have been sledgehammered to destruction in the search for booty.

Tourism and Cheap Videos

Temple images are next, as the grisly murder of the lama of Chimme Lhakhang demonstrated. There are those thieves who are already more sophisticated and calculating than the brutal band who slit the lama's throat. Near Bumthang, a temple was robbed of a priceless image by a Nepali-born con artist who represented himself to the abbot of the monastery as a would-be student. The thief pursued his religious studies long enough to become part of the community. Then one night he replaced the temple's most valuable image with a fake, and fled the country. The next day the old abbot immediately, almost instinctively, spotted the fraudulent image and spread the alarm. Remarkably, the thief was caught not long after in India trying to unload the treasure, and this story had a happy ending. But it was also a cautionary tale. Ominously, the robber later escaped while being moved from one Bhutanese jail to another. Such escapes often signal connivance.

In other South Asian nations, poverty and unemployment may be considered excuses for criminal behavior, but not in Bhutan. "We don't have beggars," said Rigzin Dorji, the scholar–civil servant who as head of the Special Commission on Cultural Affairs had the unique job of maintaining cultural standards and preserving what was called "the Bhutanese way." "Even a poor family will have a house, some chickens, maybe one or two cows, some pigs, and a little land for cultivation. The country is our mother; all the people are our children." Yet sophisticated international art thieves, on the prowl for booty from untouched monasteries and temples where literally priceless treasures are largely uncatalogued, clearly have ways of tempting even the offspring of this Himalayan Eden with windfall wealth and unusual excitement.

Innocence Lost

Bhutan has wandered without a map into that psychological territory where a magical innocence is lost and there are no signposts to what lies ahead. In Buddhist terms, the Bhutanese are collectively in some kind of *bardo*, the place between cycles of death and rebirth, waiting to see if they will enter the next life as a nation selectively modernized for the common good but otherwise unaltered, or as another small third-world country rent with social and ethnic divisions and vulnerable to corruption, violence, and political opportunism. One way or another, change is coming. . . .

Should This Life Be Saved?

Until the 1960s, the Bhutanese lived a medieval existence. There were no roads, no postal service, no telephones, no national currency or money economy, no village schools, no hospitals, no airports, no towns of any size. Families in their brightly decorated half-timbered houses grew their own food, wove the cloth for their traditional garments, and bartered what they could for a few luxuries carried into their isolated mountain valleys on the backs of traders from Tibet or India. Travel by foot or horseback was a pageant, a procession of pilgrims, entertainers, farmers, or lords making their way through snowy passes and dense forests, stopping to eat, to rest, to sing, and sometimes to dance the gentle, repetitive, slow-motion folk dances of the hills. Temples and colossal monastery-fortresses, the *dzongs*, the capitals of feudal warlords and warring regions not united under one hereditary ruler until early in [the twentieth] century, were also the centers of spiritual, legal, and even medical sustenance for all Bhutanese who could reach them. In smaller communities, monks and lamas were the sources of wisdom and healing for soul, mind, and body.

Not all of this is history, and that is part of Bhutan's dilemma. People may be healthier and better educated and have a national airline to fly them away and roads to connect them to the Asian subcontinent. But many still travel on horseback, prostrate themselves in gloriously decorated temples, and ward off the curses of evil spirits with elaborately fashioned constructions of sticks and string placed outside the family home. Should this life be saved? And how?

The Dalai Lama Writes of Spiritual Self-Confidence

by the Dalai Lama

The following selection is from a collection of teachings by the current Dalai Lama, the political and spiritual leader of Tibet. Tibet was incorporated into Communist China in 1951, and after the Chinese violently crushed a nationalist uprising in 1959, the Dalai Lama chose to go into exile. His current base is in Dharamsala in northern India. The policy of China, especially at first, was to nearly destroy the culture of independent Tibet, including its distinct version of Tantric Buddhism, and in the process thousands of monks were killed, hundreds of temples desecrated, and innumerable texts and relics destroyed. Moreover, the Chinese encouraged the mass migration of ethnic Chinese, very different from the Tibetans, into the region. Fearful that his nation's culture might completely disappear, the Dalai Lama has made it a priority to publish the teachings of Tibetan Buddhism and of his predecessor Dalai Lamas. The following selection emphasizes the importance of maintaining self-confidence in the face of the many obstacles that lie in the way of enlightenment.

The current Dalai Lama (the title means, roughly, immeasurable master or teacher) is the fourteenth to hold the position. Tibetan Buddhists believe that the

Dalai Lama is the reincarnation of Tsong-kha-pa, a reformist monk who tried to purify Tibetan Buddhism after the chaos of the Mongol Empire of the mid-1300s, and after each Dalai Lama dies, a search begins to find the new incarnation. The young boy must be born forty-nine days after the death of his predecessor, show familiarity with his predecessor's life, and be the focus of various signs and prophecies. The current Dalai Lama was named in 1935. Although Chinese authorities have made it clear that he is welcome to return to Tibet and have allowed the restoration of certain aspects of Tibetan Buddhism such as the reestablishment of temples, he remains unwilling to do so. He even admits that, given current circumstances, a fifteenth incarnation may not be necessary. Meanwhile, the Dalai Lama's teachings, his appealing personality, and the general plight of the Tibetans have made him into a sort of Buddhist celebrity around the world.

An important technique for enhancing the awakening mind is effort. Even in ordinary life we have to persevere if we are to achieve anything.

Similarly, we need to make effort in our quest for spiritual realization. When laziness takes over, our pursuit of the Dharma [Buddhist path to enlightenment] will not advance. However, it is also important to be skillful in the way we apply our effort. We have an expression in Tibetan that says that effort should be steady, like a stream of running water. Effort implies that we take an interest in whatever we are doing. In this context, it is a question of taking joy in practicing the Dharma. Perseverance does not mean making a great deal of effort at certain times and being completely lax at others. Working steadily and consistently is the key to success.

Among many obstacles, discouragement is the major stumbling block to spiritual advancement. It indicates a loss of self-esteem and a lack of confidence. In order to counter such destructive attitudes, we must generate confidence and determination. Thinking about the Buddha nature is a very positive and powerful way of doing this. All sentient beings possess the Buddha nature, the seed of enlightenment. As far as this quality is concerned, we are each on a par with everyone else. We should draw inspiration from this innate potential and keep despondency and defeatism under control.

It is also useful to think about the Buddhas of the past. They did not gain spiritual realization spontaneously. Initially, they too were like any other ordinary sentient being, miserable and tormented by sufferings and afflictions. It was only after a great deal of perseverance in the practice of the Dharma over many lifetimes that they ultimately reached the state of full enlightenment. We should draw inspiration from accounts of their lives and follow in their footsteps by embarking on a proper spiritual path. It is extremely important that we do not allow laziness or a defeatist attitude to overwhelm us. On the contrary, we should cultivate a strong sense of self-confidence and have faith in our abilities and our potential.

Avoiding Laziness

What, then, is the definition of effort? Effort here means to rejoice in doing virtuous activities. You might exert yourself in various neutral or even negative deeds, but that would not count as effort in the Buddhist sense. The practice of effort involves generating a great sense of joy in developing virtuous qualities. An obstacle to that is laziness, of which there are several kinds, such as the laziness of procrastination, the laziness of being attached to meaningless activities, and the laziness that comes from the lack of confidence in one's abilities. These obstacles should be overcome.

The purpose of the teaching of the Buddha is to transform the mind. It is just like the kind of construction we do outside, except that it takes place within. We have to determine what the necessary circumstances and materials are, accumulate them, and then begin building. Likewise, we should identify the obstructive factors and remove them one by one. The principal obstacle to developing virtuous qualities is laziness, which means not being able to get anything done. If you become attached to some meaningless activity and are unable to do spiritual practice, that is one kind of laziness. If you think you will do it tomorrow or the day after tomorrow and put it off, that is another kind of laziness. If you think, "How can a person like me achieve success in spiritual practice?" that is yet another kind of laziness.

In order to overcome laziness, we have to know the causes that bring it about. Unless you remove its causes, you will not be able to overcome laziness. These causes include being fond of whiling away your time, becoming attached to too much relaxation or too much sleep, and not being dismayed by the sufferings of the cycle of existence. These are the three principal factors giving rise to laziness. The more you recognize the faults and sufferings of the cycle of existence, the stronger will be your attempt to overcome them. On the other hand, if you do not see the sufferings of the cycle of existence and if you feel happy as you are, you will not attempt to free yourself from them. As the great Indian scholar and adept Aryadeva said, "How can someone who is not discouraged by the faults of the cycle of existence take interest in nirvana? Like leaving home, it is also hard to leave worldly existence."

The disturbing emotions are compared to a kind of net. Once you fall into this net and are caught, you will be unable to free yourself from the hold of the disturbing emotions and you will fall into the jaws of death. One of the ways to counter laziness is to think about impermanence and the nature of death. Death has no compassion. Gradually, one by one, death takes us all. We constantly hear that someone has died in such and such a place or that someone has died on this or that road. Normally, when we hear about someone else's death, we tend to think that it was their turn to die and our turn will never come. We are like those foolish sheep whose companions are being led into the slaughterhouse but who still do not understand that they too are about to die. With no fear of death, we will simply go on enjoying ourselves and looking forward to sleep. When death will strike is unknown. It may be that death will visit you when you have just begun some undertaking. It makes no difference to death whether someone has just started some project or has half completed it. Death can catch us unawares at any time. But since we are going to die soon, while we are still alive we must try to accumulate merit. Once death overtakes us, it will be too late to eliminate laziness. At that time nothing can be done. Therefore, do not procrastinate. Do not put spiritual practice off until tomorrow or the next day; start immediately.

Awareness of Death

If you always procrastinate, putting off what you have to do until tomorrow or next year, even making a list of things you are going to do and, these days, storing it in your computer, one day you may suddenly be struck by a fatal illness. You will have to visit the hospital and take those awful medicines that you do not want to take. The surgeons may operate on you. Sometimes these white-clothed figures may be kind and compassionate; sometimes they operate on you as if they were simply opening up a machine that has no feelings.

Normally, when people are healthy and free from illness, they can boast that they do not believe in past or future lives. But as death looms, you recollect all your misdeeds. Your mind will be filled with remorse, pain, and unhappiness. You might even hear the sounds of hell nearby and wet your bed with fear. An acquaintance told me that when he was suffering a very severe sickness and in great pain, he heard many strange sounds and voices. Sometimes people faint with pain. Then, before coming around, it seems many people have an experience like traveling through a tunnel. That is when they have what are called near-death experiences. People who have accumulated severe negative deeds encounter many frightening experiences as a result of the dissolution of the various physical elements of their bodies. When those who have accumulated a great deal of virtue are faced with the process of dying, they experience a sense of satisfaction and happiness.

Now, while we are still alive, we might be driven from our country by our enemies, but we still expect to be reunited with our relatives at some time. But at the time of death, you have to part from your friends and relatives forever. Even this precious body that has accompanied you everywhere will be taken from you. And once it is dead, people see your body as something dangerous, fearful, and horrible. That is why some great yogins [meditation masters] have said that the frightful dead body is with us always, even while we are alive. You should see your human life as a vessel to cross the great ocean of suffering. Such a vessel will be very difficult to find in the future, so having found such a precious opportunity, in your bewilderment you should not just sleep.

The sublime teaching of the Buddha is a cause of infinite joy and happiness, but what could be more unfortunate than giving up this supreme path and getting distracted by causes leading to suffering? Take control of yourself, put procrastination behind you, and try to accumulate merit and wisdom to make your body and mind suitable for spiritual practice. This is comparable to preparing for war. First you must generate the self-confidence to fight. You must be determined to undergo all hardships and gain victory over all obstructive forces. Just as a military leader needs a strong force of well-armed, well-equipped, brave men, you should accumulate merit and wisdom. When you fight you should put your weapons to full use, aimed directly at the enemy. Likewise, whatever spiritual path you practice, you must wield the weapon of wisdom with mindfulness and attention. Consequently, you will defeat the enemy, laziness, and gain control over your body and mind, making it easier to engage in virtuous practice. To think that you have no capacity, intelligence, or potential is a great fault. Even in ordinary life you must have self-confidence to do whatever it is you want to do. People in the West are subject to what is called low self-esteem. I do not know whether it is present in Tibetan society or other cultures, but low self-esteem is very debilitating. Whether you are concerned with spiritual practice or the work of ordinary life, you must maintain confidence.

Determination to Follow the Dharma Brings Happiness

The Kadampa [an early Tibetan Buddhist sect from about A.D. 1000] masters of the past had nothing to enjoy in their dry caves. They were so determined in their spiritual practice that they stayed there confidently and happily. They employed their entire being—their body, speech, and mind—in the practice of the Dharma. They never feared that because of their Dharma practice they would run out of food or other facilities and die. The Kadampa masters would think that even if they had to become beggars, they would rather pray for death than let themselves waste their time not practicing the Dharma. There is a danger of worrying that if you die, who will help you? Who will pray for you? But the Kadampa masters used to think, "Why should I bother whether someone helps me or not? I should prefer to die a natural death in a bare and empty cave just as animals and birds do." This is the kind of determination with which they would engage in their practice. They would say, "If I'm treated like an outcast, I will voluntarily accept it. If I have to join the company of dogs, I will do that. Like a dog I will wander here and there in pursuit of Dharma." Because of their determination they would finally attain Buddhahood.

If you are really going to practice the Dharma, you need strong determination and self-confidence. If you have no self-confidence, you will not achieve anything.

Without expectation or doubt, enter into spiritual practice. Read the life of Milarepa [a Tibetan Buddhist saint, 1040–1123]. He gave up everything: his friends, his relatives, his possessions. In one of his famous songs he says, "If I fall sick unknown to my relatives and if I die unknown to my enemies, I, the yogin, will have fulfilled my wish." Even when we are concerned with fulfilling our responsibilities to one person or a few individuals, we have to have determination. Naturally, when we are cultivating the awakening mind, whose aim is the happiness of all sentient beings, we need especially strong determination.

If you say you want to cultivate the awakening mind for the sake of all sentient beings, but at the same time you say you do not feel capable, there is a contradiction. Generating mental courage does not mean you have to be proud. Pride and self-confidence are two different things. When you cultivate positive qualities like love, compassion, and the awakening mind, you should do so with self-confidence. The awakening mind is driven by the force of compassion, by concern for the welfare of all sentient beings. You are no longer bound by an ignorant misconception of self. You can wholeheartedly fight the disturbing emotions with confidence and determination.

Buddhist Courage and Tibet's Fate

With regard to the cause of Tibet, we must always think that we can succeed. We should have self-confidence. Let me tell you a story. Around 1979, during one of the more lenient periods when Tibetans were able to come and visit their relatives in exile, one man came to talk to me. He had been born in Lhasa [Tibet's capital] and had lived there in the 1950s and witnessed the uprising. He told me that the Chinese are extremely clever and that their population is huge. They have so many weapons that there is nothing we can do. He was completely discouraged. I think the sound of weapons being fired in the 1950s was still in his ears. Then there was an old monk from the Dokham area. He had seen the military operations being carried out in those areas. Whole villages were wiped out, and many people were massacred. I told him that when we are so few and they are so many, these things will definitely take place. Then I asked him what would happen if one Tibetan were to fight one Chinese. He laughed and said that then it would be easy, that we could play with them in the palms of our hands. That was his kind of mental courage. It is not a matter of pride, but it is important to have self-confidence, to think that you can do it. When problems arose in 1959, we Tibetans were in a very difficult position. The entire Tibetan population is only 6 million, so things were quite discouraging. But since 1959 we have never given up, because we are fighting for a true cause, a just cause. We have never lost our determination to achieve our aim. Even though more than forty years have passed since the Communist Chinese first came to Tibet, instead of disappearing, the Tibetan cause is gaining momentum. We are getting more support, and there is a possibility of achieving something before long.

How can we maintain self-confidence and not let ourselves get discouraged? The compassionate Buddha, who tells only the truth and nothing else, has put it this way. Even those sentient beings living an inferior kind of life, like bees, flies, and other insects, whose physical existence is weak, have the Buddha nature. If they make the effort, even such weak sentient beings can evolve over many lifetimes and ultimately achieve the unsurpassable state of Buddhahood, so difficult to attain. This is what the Buddha taught. All sentient beings possessing a luminous mind have the potential to attain Buddhahood. However weak they may be, and no matter how overwhelming the suffering they encounter, they all have the potential to attain Buddhahood. If this is so, when we have been born as human beings and know to some extent what is beneficial and what is harmful, if we do not give up the practices of a bodhisattva, why should we not attain Buddhahood?

Buddhist Communities in the United States Are Large and Diverse

by Diana L. Eck

Buddhism first arrived in the United States during the California gold rush of the mid-1800s when Chinese immigrants crossed the Pacific Ocean to work in the goldfields and on the railway lines. In the late 1800s Japanese immigrants followed. Both communities continued to practice their varied forms of the Buddhist faith. And when the U.S. government changed its immigration laws in 1965 in ways that allowed millions of Asians to enter the country, these Buddhist communities expanded and others took root. Notable large communities of Buddhists to emerge in the last decades have been those of the so-called overseas Chinese, from Taiwan and Hong Kong, and the millions of Vietnamese who made their way to the United States after the Vietnam War. There are also groups of Buddhists, all maintaining their distinct versions of the faith, from Korea, Sri Lanka, Thailand, Cambodia, Laos, and Tibet. Meanwhile, many European Americans have adopted Buddhist teachings and have joined these communities or founded their own.

In the following selection, Diana L. Eck examines how one community of Chinese Buddhists in Southern

California has developed a version of the faith that is particularly relevant to immigrants and has grown to have an influence on not only local but national politics. She goes on to describe how this group represents only one strand of the diversity of Buddhism in the contemporary United States. Diana L. Eck is a professor of comparative religion and Indian studies at Harvard University.

The Buddha's Birthday is celebrated for weeks on end in Los Angeles. More than three hundred Buddhist temples sit in this great city facing the Pacific, and every weekend for most of the month of May the Buddha's Birthday is observed somewhere, by some group —the Vietnamese at a community college in Orange County, the Japanese at their temples in central Los Angeles, the pan-Buddhist Sangha Council at a Korean temple in downtown L.A. My introduction to the Buddha's Birthday observance was at Hsi Lai Temple in Hacienda Heights, just east of Los Angeles. It is said to be the largest Buddhist temple in the Western hemisphere, built by Chinese Buddhists hailing originally from Taiwan and advocating a progressive Humanistic Buddhism dedicated to the positive transformation of the world. In an upscale Los Angeles suburb with its malls, doughnut shops, and gas stations, I was about to pull over and ask for directions when the road curved up a hill, and suddenly there it was—an opulent red and gold cluster of sloping tile rooftops like a radiant vision from another world, completely dominating the vista. The ornamental gateway read "International Buddhist Progress Society," the name under which the temple is incorporated, and I gazed up in amazement. This was in 1991, and I had never seen anything like it in America.

The entrance took me first into the Bodhisattva Hall of gilded images and rich lacquerwork, where five of the great bodhisattvas of the Mahayana Buddhist tradition receive the prayers of the faithful. The bodhisattvas are the enlightened and compassionate beings who come to the threshold of nirvana or enlightenment and yet choose to remain in the world of birth and death to help others along the path. Among them I recognized the popular Kuan Yin, carrying a branch of willow and a vessel, often approached for the blessings of health and beneficence. I moved with the stream of Chinese families into the huge open-air fieldstone courtyard that is the center of the temple and monastery complex. It was brilliantly alive with hundreds of people dressed in their festive best. Across the courtyard was the broad staircase leading up to the main Buddha Hall. For the occasion of the Buddha's Birthday and the afternoon garden party that was to accompany the celebration, a dozen American flags were posted on either side of the staircase, snapping in the blue May morning. I climbed the stairs, turning every few steps to view the scene. Ten minutes ago I had been driving down Main Street, U.S.A., and now my vision of America was in radical transformation.

In the Buddha Hall, more than four hundred people were on their knees on red cushioned kneelers. The room was resonant with chanting. In the front rows were the many black-robed nuns who are the backbone of Hsi Lai and behind them the multicolored multitude of Chinese families. The whole hall was standing, bowing, kneeling. Gongs resounded, bells tinkled. I took a seat along a side bench and began to absorb the magnificence of this great Buddha Hall.

On the high altar were three large, seated, golden Buddhas. In the center was Shakyamuni, the historical Buddha, whose birthday was being observed today. He was born a prince, Siddhartha Gautama, in the foothills of the Himalayas. Despite the comfort of his palace life, he was disturbed by the suffering of sickness, old age, and death and set out from the palace to find the cause of suffering and the path to freedom from suffering. To one side sat Amitabha or Amida, the Buddha of Infinite Light, who attained enlightenment and vowed to create a Pure Land where people may be reborn and attain peace. On the other side sat the Medicine Buddha, whose vows on behalf of humanity included the healing of body and mind. The walls of the great hall were covered with thousands of small Buddhas, each lit by a tiny light and bearing the name of a donor. In the Mahayana tradition of East Asia it becomes clear that the awakened mind of enlightenment cannot be limited to one historical Buddha but is potentially infinite.

In front of me, a four-year-old girl with a ponytail knelt beside her mother, watching her carefully, peeking up to her side to see if she had done it right. Bowing, her mother turned her palms upward as if to receive blessings from above. Now, the child was turning her tiny palms upward too, learning the forms of prayer that come with centuries of tradition. To me, and perhaps to this child, the whole universe seemed filled with the rolling rhythm of chanting and the movement of hundreds of people at prayer. Here, as in so much of the Buddhist tradition, it is not silence but chanting that brings the heart and mind to stillness.

The Buddha's Birthday

As the chanting subsided, I heard a woman's voice on the loudspeaker announcing the significance of this occasion. "Two thousand five hundred thirty-five years ago the Buddha was born in the Lumbini Garden in present-day Nepal. The Buddha is like a lamp in this world of suffering, shining the way for us. Today we have a special ceremony in which we symbolically bathe the image of the Baby Buddha. In bathing the Baby Buddha, we also purify defilements such as greed and anger that are within ourselves." As she spoke, people began to rise and line up for this simple ceremony. I fell in line with the mother and her ponytailed daughter. They were from a nearby suburb that is now more than half Chinese. It was her first Buddha's Birthday, in fact her first time at the temple. The announcer continued, "The pure nature of the Buddha is innate in us all. It is covered up with these defilements. We need to clean off the dirt so that we can shine. When the sun is covered by clouds, we are unable to see the sun shining. So when we bathe the Buddha, keep in mind that what we want to purify is our own defilements, so that our pure nature can shine." She concluded, "If you would like to transfer the merits of this act to others, you are invited to do so." This is the Buddhist practice of engaging in an act of faith or charity, all the while asking that the credit for the action be put on someone else's account.

Near the door of the Buddha Hall, a small standing image of Baby Buddha with his right hand lifted heavenward was set in a basin inside a beautiful flower-decked pagoda. According to the accounts of miracles that attended the Buddha's birth, the child was born standing up, and at his birth the heavens burst forth with a shower of flowers. Each person approached the

Baby Buddha, bowed, and took one of the long-handled bamboo ladles to scoop up the liquid from the basin and pour it over the infant's shoulders. The woman next to me told me it was sweetened tea, and indeed I could see that the same liquid was being handed out in cups for all to sip. I helped lift her four-year-old high enough to grasp the bamboo ladle for herself and pour her sweet offering over the Baby Buddha. As I held her up, my mind was a rush of thoughts. I wondered what the Buddha would mean to the girl as she becomes part of the energetic, homogenizing, diversifying combustion of American culture. I wondered if this place and the tradition it embodies would become important parts of her life, if she would come here for classes or meditation, if she would become involved as a young adult and seek the advice of the nuns, or if she would come to the temple only to observe the death of an uncle, a grandfather, or her mother. Or she might espouse secular values and never return at all. As I took the bamboo ladle myself, I quietly prayed to transfer whatever merit I might gain from this offering to her.

Hsi Lai means "Coming to the West," meaning the journey of Buddhism to America. Of course, from the standpoint of Asia, Buddhism has moved steadily eastward from India through Central Asia, to China, Japan, and Korea, and now across the Pacific to America. But in the global scope of things, America is still seen as the "West." This temple was built by and is linked to a mountaintop temple-monastic complex in Taiwan called Fo Kuang Shan, the center of the Humanistic Buddhist movement guided by its founder, Master Hsing Yün. The temple here sits on fourteen acres, the building complex alone being over one hundred thousand square feet and costing some thirty million dollars. It has a membership of more than twenty thousand, drawn largely from the Chinese immigrant community from Taiwan, making it on a scale with the largest of America's new megachurches. Surveying the whole from the top of the grand staircase, I looked down on the courtyard surrounded by a large compound of monastic residences homing nearly one hundred monastics, mostly nuns. Across the court were a conference center with an auditorium and facilities for simultaneous translation; a museum of Buddhist ritual and visual arts; and a library of some fifty thousand volumes. At the periphery of the building was an impressive bookstore of Buddhist books in English and Chinese, cassettes, prayer beads, incense, and images; and beneath us was a large cafeteria specializing in vegetarian food.

Resistance to Temple Building

The very existence of this temple is a tremendous achievement. While my new ponytailed friend will take for granted a landscape that includes Hsi Lai and other spectacular Chinese Buddhist temples, this was not part of the religious landscape of California even twenty years ago. It took some five years to gain the zoning clearances to build here. Townspeople were stunned by the news that a large Chinese temple would be built on the hillside, and they turned up in droves at zoning meetings determined to thwart the project. Dozens of meetings took place, both public and private, with promises and compromises on all sides. Finally, the cornerstone was laid in 1986, and by the end of 1989 the building was dedicated—on Thanksgiving Day. Still, it took time to win a place as citizens in Hacienda Heights. The next year a float created by the temple for

the Fourth of July parade was met with boos and heck-
ling along the parade route. After that, the temple began a series of initiatives to build bridges with these
new neighbors—food baskets for the needy on Thanksgiving and Christmas, invitations to the whole commu-

*Worshippers pray at this Buddha statue at a Japanese tea garden in San
Francisco. Buddhist communities are flourishing in the United States.*

nity to come to dinner at the temple in the days preceding big events like the Buddha's Birthday or Chinese New Year. The temple also invited outside groups to use its conference room facilities, and community groups took them up on it. The outreach seems to have been a success. By 1991 five hundred people from the community accepted the invitation to the Chinese New Year community banquet.

The Buddha's Birthday was a day for the family. Multicolored helium balloons floated aloft bearing the temple's insignia; at food stalls around the courtyard tickets could be exchanged for spring rolls, fried rice, shrimp, and delicacies. In the reception room, individuals and families consulted with nuns regarding questions from their daily lives. I spent the day eating and talking. From Venerable I-Han I got a glimpse of the strength and grit of the nuns who had been virtually at the helm of this multimillion dollar construction project. From Venerable Yun-Kai I heard about the outreach programs of the temple—teaching meditation at a hospital drug dependency center, visiting inmates at the Terminal Island Penitentiary, conducting weekend classes for children, arranging meditation retreats for non-Chinese seekers.

The Venerable Man-Ya explained to me the vision of Master Hsing Yün's Humanistic Buddhism. "It revolves around the needs of people," she said. "He speaks of building the Pure Land on earth, not simply looking beyond this life to Amitabha's heavenly Pure Land." She explained that many Chinese people expect Buddhism will be important to them only at the time of someone's death, when they will call monks or nuns to chant and when they will come to the temple for special rites. But Master Hsing Yün insists that the Buddha's teachings are concerned with the living, not just the dead. The ebullience of this temple seems a confirmation of that vision. Man-Ya sat at a table just outside the Buddha Hall, and as we talked she signed people up for the Three Refuges ceremony. Participants would affirm their faith in the three great "treasures," by taking refuge in the Buddha, the Dharma, and the Sangha—the teacher, the teachings, and the community of Buddhists. Taking refuge in these three treasures is the formal act of affirming one's participation in the Buddhist tradition, and the list for the afternoon ceremony was many pages long.

By the end of the day, I had begun to realize that the serious social vision of Buddhist Humanism was combined here at Hsi Lai with the sheer happiness of having created a landmark center for the Chinese Buddhist community in America. The community was justly proud of this place, but learning the ropes of participation in American life would pose some difficulties.

A Vice-Presidential Visit

Five years later, Hsi Lai became the focal point of a presidential campaign finance controversy when Vice President Al Gore visited the temple in the 1996 election campaign. Was it a civic luncheon that he attended or a fund-raiser? In October of 1996 the story began to break. As a *Washington Post* writer put it, "With its pagoda-style ochre roofs and red-pillared Hall of the Buddha and robed monks wandering piously through Oriental gardens, the Hsi Lai Temple seems more like an island of spiritual tranquility in this bustling Los Angeles suburb than the focal point of a growing controversy over questionable big-money contributions to a presidential re-election campaign." But controversy there was, and the temple that had reached out to become involved in civic life was now at the center of a public dispute. It was alleged that the event was a fund-raiser, in which case it was illegal for a tax-exempt religious institution. Distressed members of the lay temple community responded to the controversy with a statement expressing their "sadness" at the allegations. "For years, Hsi Lai Temple has been our second home and we have an intimate understanding of the temple's operations." They characterized the event as a "civic luncheon" and recalled how the vice president spoke movingly about learning from one another, respecting one another's traditions, and cooperating "to offer the best resources of our minds and hearts to the United States." The vice president's speech there had praised the practice of placing one's palms together as a gesture of greeting. He said, "The placing of palms together is very much in the American spirit. To bring together one, two, three, four, so many, is simply wonderful. It is an act of cooperation, union, mutual respect, and harmony."

This group of temple members explained what even a brief visit to Hsi Lai makes clear: that this is a Chinese temple community trying very hard to undertake the most American of activities, that is, participation in civic life. They wrote,

> Trying to westernize Buddhism and do more to benefit the American people, Hsi Lai Temple monastics have chosen to be actively engaged in American society. For example, they have helped the American Heart Association with the annual Heart Run; they have given lectures on Buddhist teachings in response to invitations by colleges and universities; they have invited local religious groups to participate in New Year's Peace Services; they have held a wide variety of charity events and recycling drives;

they have joined Fourth of July parades and celebrations; they have shared joy with the community through our Chinese New Year community outreach event. The invitation to the Vice President was also done out of the same understanding, as a way for cultural integration and exchange of friendship.

Far from coming to know the Hsi Lai Temple through its impressive achievements, most Americans first learned of it through this oft-revisited controversy. For this Buddhist community, the learning curve on America's strict view of the separation of church and state was steep, and yet some felt that their temple had been unfairly criticized because they were Chinese. Clearly, in its first decade, Hsi Lai Temple has experienced the full range of "coming to the West," from zoning hearings to gala celebrations to hot political controversy.

Many Buddhisms

As impressive as it is, Hsi Lai Temple is only a small part of the American Buddhist story. In the past thirty years Buddhism has come to America to stay, with Buddhists from all over Asia—Koreans and Chinese, Vietnamese and Cambodians, Thais, Tibetans, and Sri Lankans. Nowhere can we see the whole panorama of Buddhism as clearly as in Los Angeles.

I had the usual East Coast stereotypes of Los Angeles as a sprawling, smoggy city with no center and no periphery, but when I went to L.A. to do research on Buddhism in America, I discovered a city I came to love. Of course, all I really know of L.A. is its Asian religious life, which is every bit as ebullient and astonishing as its world of entertainment. L.A. is unquestionably the most complex Buddhist city in the world, with its vast variety of Buddhist temples and meditation centers representing the whole spectrum of Asian, and now American, Buddhism. Wat Thai in North Hollywood anchors two generations of Thai immigrants, and Kwan Um Sah on Western Avenue gathers Korean Buddhists in a former Masonic hall, its plush red-carpeted chamber now the shrine room for gilded images of the Buddha. In Long Beach there are Cambodian temples, the largest in a former union hall, and in Orange County dozens of suburban homes have become the temple centers of a large Vietnamese community. The elegant Jodo Shinshu Temple in South Central L.A. is one of several temples that serve third- and fourth-generation Japanese Americans. In Los Angeles, Buddhists who would never have met one another in Asia find themselves neighbors, often with very different cultural experiences of Buddhism. Like so many other religious traditions, seemingly coherent wholes from the outside, the Buddhist tradition becomes more variegated and complex the more closely one looks.

The Asian forms of Buddhism are only half the story, for there has also been a turn toward Buddhism on the part of native-born Euro-Americans and even African and Hispanic Americans. The Zen Center of Los Angeles, occupying half a city block, answers its busy phone lines with an array of automated options: sittings, retreats, study groups, evening Dharma talks, directions to the center. And there are a dozen other Zen centers in the area. The Tibetan Dharmadhatu Center, the Vipassana sitting groups, and the International Buddhism Meditation Center provide homes for various forms of Buddhist practice that have attracted native-born Americans. The Soka Gakkai International, a group with strong roots in Japan and an active mission outreach, has its American headquarters in Santa Monica.

Buddhist Los Angeles

In the 1950s one might have mistaken the Beat Zen of the counterculture for a fad that would fade, but with each succeeding decade Buddhism has become more vibrant. Today Buddhism has given its own distinctive hues to the tapestry of American religious life. Its traditions of meditation appeal to frank, practical Americans. As teachers in American Dharma centers often say, Buddhism is not a set of beliefs to be taken on faith but a set of observations about life, the sources of suffering, and the end of suffering to be tested in our own experience. Even more, it is a set of practices that enable people to cultivate the equanimity, mental clarity, and self-awareness needed to observe clearly, in their own experience, whether or not these postulates are true. "Come and see," is the invitation. For the past three decades, Americans in unprecedented numbers have accepted the invitation. They have tried it out, and whether they have ended up calling themselves Buddhists or not, many have stuck with it. By 1997 more than a thousand Buddhist meditation and practice centers were listed in the new edition of *The Complete Guide to Buddhist America*. Los Angeles has its fair share, to be sure, but there are also centers in Elk Rapids, Michigan, and Omaha, Nebraska. No part of the United States today is untouched by the presence of this form of Buddhism based in meditation practice.

The past three decades have not only brought Buddhist immigrants from all over Asia in unprecedented numbers, they have also seen ancient lineages of Buddhist teaching, passed from teacher to disciple in Asia for over twenty-five hundred years, cross the Pacific to America. The torch of teaching has been handed to a new generation of non-Asian teachers, many of whom are women, almost all of whom are laity. Few monastics are among them, so they are more likely to be dressed in slacks and T-shirts than saffron or gray robes. They teach in living rooms and conference centers, hospitals and prisons, elegant urban centers and mountain retreat centers. In their style and language, in their social and environmental activism, they are slowly but surely developing something we can call American Buddhism.

Here in America, Buddhists from all over the world are discovering their own diversity, their many Buddhisms. Not surprisingly, a gulf of experience and understanding separates the old Chinese and Japanese immigrant communities, some of whom have been in the U.S. for nearly one hundred years, and the new Thai, Vietnamese, Cambodian, and Chinese immigrant communities just getting started. Another separates the first-generation immigrants and their American-born children, who straddle the culture of Buddhist temple enclaves and the culture of their American high schools and colleges. Wide differences also separate Asian Buddhists who light incense and shake fortune sticks before the Buddha altar and American-born meditation practitioners who may consider such rituals extraneous to the teachings of the Buddha. Buddhism in America today is experiencing its own internal struggles with pluralism as cultures and generations express their different understandings of what it means to be Buddhist.

Glossary

ahimsa: Nonviolence.

Amitabha: A buddha associated with Pure Land Buddhism.

arhat: A Buddhist saint who remains "lower" than a full Buddha; used in Theravada Buddhism.

Ashoka: An emperor of India (reigned 273–232 B.C.) renowned for spreading Buddhism.

Avalokiteshvara: The bodhisattva of compassion also known as Avalokita.

bhikku: A Buddhist monk.

bhikkuni: A Buddhist nun.

bodhi: Enlightenment or awakening.

Bodhidharma: The fifth-century founder of Ch'an, or Zen, Buddhism.

bodhisattva: A figure who strives to attain buddhahood; literally, "awakened being." In Mahayana Buddhism a bodhisattva is one who has achieved enlightenment but, instead of entering nirvana, chooses to remain in the world to help others.

Buddha: An enlightened soul; usually used to refer to Siddhartha Gautama, after he achieved enlightenment.

Dalai Lama: A highly enlightened monk who serves as the spiritual leader of Tibetan Buddhism and the exiled political leader of Tibet.

dharma (*dhamma*): The Buddhist path; also, Buddhist teachings or truth.

dhyana: Meditation.

dukha: Suffering.

eightfold path: The characteristics that, once mastered, help one to overcome desire and, therefore, suffering: right views, right thinking, right speech, right action, right way of life, right endeavor, right mindfulness, and right meditation.

four noble truths: The basic teachings of Buddhism outlined in the Buddha's first sermons. They are as follows: Suffering is a keynote of existence; suffering is caused by desire or, more accurately, by attachment to desire; suffering can be overcome by doing away with desire; and to overcome suffering, one must follow the eightfold path.

guru: A religious teacher.

Hinayana: The "smaller path" of Buddhism; the term was used by Mahayana Buddhists to refer, disparagingly, to the original Buddhist sects that appeared in India in the centuries after the Buddha's death, and later was applied to Theravada Buddhists.

karma: The consequences of earthly action.

koan: A lesson taking the form of a riddle or paradox used in Zen meditation.

Kuan Yin: A bodhisattva popular in China and elsewhere in east Asia. Derived from the Indian Avalokiteshvara, the bodhisattva of compassion, Kuan Yin was later feminized into the Chinese "goddess" of mercy and good fortune.

lama: A Tibetan Buddhist monk.

Mahayana: The "greater path" of Buddhism practiced in many forms in China, Korea, Japan, Vietnam, and Tibet.

Maitreya: A buddha who some Buddhists believe will in the future appear as the successor to Gautama Buddha.

mandala: A "sacred circle" used in Buddhist rituals in Tibet.

mantra: A chant made up of a series of repeated words or syllables that is intended to focus the mind during meditation.

Mara: The force of temptation or of death; often personified as a god in Buddhist art and mythology.

maya: Illusion; the world.

nirvana: The state of being released from the wheel of birth and death; the great peace that is the ultimate goal of Buddhists.

Pali: The Indian language in which many of the early Buddhist texts were written.

prajna: Wisdom or insight; understanding of the true, transitory nature of the world and of worldly things.

Pure Land: A Buddhist school preaching an otherworldly paradise presided over by a buddha named Amitabha. The goal of devotion in this school is to be reborn in the Pure Land.

Sakyamuni: The sage of the Sakyas (an ancient Indian tribal dynasty); another name for Siddhartha Gautama, the Buddha.

samadhi: The focused concentration that is the goal of Buddhist meditation.

samsara: The wheel of existence; reincarnation.

Sangha: The Buddhist community; an order of Buddhist monks or nuns.

satori: A Japanese word for a flash of insight or a glimpse of enlightenment; the goal of Zen meditation.

skandhas: The five conditions that characterize the self: the body, feeling, conception, personality, and consciousness. Having great attachment to the five *skandhas* ensures continued reincarnation.

stupa: A holy mound or shrine.

Tantra: A form of Buddhism emphasizing ritual and magic.

tathagata: An enlightened soul; a Theravada saint.

Theravada: The "teachings of the elders"; the smaller path of Buddhism also referred to as Hinayana and practiced in Sri Lanka and Southeast Asia. Strictly speaking, the Theravada was just one of the Hinayana schools; the term is used to avoid the disparaging nature of the term *Hinayana*.

Tripitaka: The "three baskets" of early Buddhist scripture. Written in the ancient Indian language of Pali, the Tripitaka consists of the Vinaya (rules for monks), the Sutta (teachings), and the Abhidamma (supplementary doctrines).

Vinaya: Rules for Buddhist monastic orders.

wu: The Chinese word for enlightenment.

Zen: The Japanese word for *dhyana*, or meditation; a popular school of Mahayana Buddhism known originally in China as Ch'an.

Chronology

B.C.

623–543

The life of Siddhartha Gautama, the original Buddha and founder of Buddhism, according to Theravada Buddhism.

565–486

The life of the Buddha according to Mahayana Buddhism.

490–410

The life of the Buddha according to recent scholarly research.

480

The First Buddhist Council takes place in Rajagha in northern India (according to Mahayana tradition). There, Buddhist disciples organize the original Buddha's teachings into a set of repetitive oral chants. These form the *Tripitaka*, or "three baskets" of knowledge passed down by the Buddha.

350

The Second Buddhist council takes place in Vaisali in northern India. There, Buddhist leaders settle on a collection of classic teachings that go beyond the Tripitaka, but they also argue over whether the Buddha's original teachings might be too difficult or severe.

273–232

Ashoka, the Indian emperor who converted to Buddhism,

reigns. His efforts help turn Buddhism into an organized religion and encourage it to spread.

250
The Third Buddhist Council takes place at Pataliputra, Ashoka's capital. It confirms the teachings of Theravada Buddhism.

247
Ashoka's son Mahinda takes Buddhism to Sri Lanka.

ca. 200
The first Mahayana Buddhist schools are formed in India.

89–77
The classical canon of Buddhist texts is written down for the first time in Sri Lanka using the Pali language.

A.D.
ca. 100
The Fourth Buddhist Council, held in northwestern India, results in a split between Mahayana and Theravada Buddhism.

100–250
Missionaries take Buddhism to China, Central Asia, Burma, Cambodia, Laos, and Vietnam.

350–414
Buddhist texts are translated into Chinese.

372
Buddhism appears in Korea.

400–500
Pure Land Buddhism arises in China. Buddhism takes hold in the islands of what is now Indonesia.

526

The founder of Zen (Ch'an) Buddhism, Bodhidharma, arrives in southern China from India.

538

Buddhism arrives in Japan, becoming the state religion in 594.

641–650

The first Buddhist temples are erected in Tibet.

750–780

The Borobudur temple complex is built on the Indonesian island of Java.

845

Buddhists suffer persecution from China's Tang dynasty rulers.

868

The first printed book appears in China. It is the Mahayana classic the *Diamond Sutra*.

1100–1200

Pure Land and Zen Buddhist schools thrive in Japan.

1113–1150

Angkor Wat is built by the Cambodian Khmer Empire.

1193

Islamic conquerors crush Bihar, the center of Buddhism in India, destroying monasteries and schools. The conquest effectively removes Buddhism from the land of its birth, and many Indian Buddhists migrate to Nepal, Bhutan, and other Himalayan mountain kingdoms.

1357

Tsong-kha-pa, founder of the Yellow Hat order of Tibetan Buddhism, is born.

1360

Theravada Buddhism becomes the state religion in Thailand. It soon dominates Laos and Cambodia as well.

1400–1550

The great era of Zen aesthetics occurs in Japan, featuring great accomplishments in painting and poetry as well as the development of the tea ceremony.

1578

The fifth leader, or lama, of Tibet's Yellow Hat sect becomes the official Dalai Lama.

1757

British colonial possession of India begins. British India later includes both Sri Lanka and Burma.

1853

Chinese immigrants build the first Buddhist temple in the United States in San Francisco.

1863

France begins to take colonial possession of Vietnam, Cambodia, and Laos, a process that continues for several decades.

1880

Western theosophists travel to India to study Buddhism.

1907

The Buddhist Society of Great Britain is founded.

1952

The World Fellowship of Buddhism is founded.

1956

Buddhists around the world celebrate the twenty-five-hundredth year of their faith. Religious leaders use the event to call for cooperation and understanding among the many Buddhist sects and make an effort to revive Buddhism in India.

1959

The fourteenth Dalai Lama flees to India following the Chinese takeover of Tibet.

1960s–1990s

Changes in immigration laws and the end of European colonial empires result in many Buddhists moving to the United States, Canada, Great Britain, and other Western nations.

1963

Vietnamese Buddhist monks protest corruption and war in their country. A number of them burn themselves to death.

1965

The first Theravada Buddhist monastery is built in the United States.

1989

The Dalai Lama receives the Nobel Peace Prize.

For Further Research

Books

Anne Bancroft, ed., *The Dhammapada.* Rockport, MA: Element, 1997.

Norma Bixler, *Burmese Journey.* Yellow Springs, OH: Antioch, 1967.

John Blofeld, *Bodhisattva of Compassion: The Mystical Tradition of Kuan Yin.* Boulder, CO: Shambhala, 1978.

———, *The Wheel of Life: The Autobiography of a Western Buddhist.* Boston: Shambhala, 1988.

E.A. Burtt, ed., *Teachings of the Compassionate Buddha.* New York: Mentor, 1959.

Michael Carrithers, *The Buddha: A Very Short Introduction.* Oxford, England: Oxford University Press, 1996.

Thomas Cleary, ed. and trans., *Zen Antics: A Hundred Stories of Enlightenment.* Boston: Shambhala, 1993.

Edward Conze, trans., *Buddhist Scriptures.* London: Penguin, 1982.

———, trans., *Buddhist Wisdom Books.* New York: Harper and Row, 1972.

Barbara Crossette, *So Close to Heaven: The Vanishing Buddhist Kingdoms of the Himalayas.* New York: Knopf, 1995.

Dalai Lama, *The Joy of Living and Dying in Peace.* Ed. Donald S. Lopez Jr. San Francisco: HarperSanFrancisco, 1997.

David M. Davies, *The Rice Bowl of Asia.* South Brunswick, NJ: A.S. Barnes, 1967.

William Theodore de Bary, ed., *The Buddhist Tradition in India, China, and Japan*. New York: Vintage, 1972.

Heinrich Dumoulin and John C. Maraldo, *Buddhism in the Modern World*. New York: Macmillan, 1976.

H. Byron Earhart, *Japanese Religion: Unity and Diversity*. 3rd ed. Belmont, CA: Wadsworth, 1982.

Diana L. Eck, *A New Religious America: How a "Christian Country" Has Become the World's Most Religiously Diverse Nation*. San Francisco: HarperSanFrancisco, 2001.

W.Y. Evans-Wentz, trans., *The Tibetan Book of the Dead*. 3rd ed. Oxford, England: Oxford University Press, 1960.

René Grousset, *In the Footsteps of the Buddha*. London: Routledge and Kegan Paul, 1932.

Heinrich Harrer, *Seven Years in Tibet*. New York: Dutton, 1954.

Christmas Humphreys, *Buddhism*. Harmondsworth, UK: Penguin, 1951.

Louise Hunter, *Buddhism in Hawaii: Its Impact on a Yankee Community*. Honolulu: University of Hawaii Press, 1971.

Robert C. Lester, *Theravada Buddhism in Southeast Asia*. Ann Arbor: University of Michigan Press, 1973.

Trevor Ling, *The Buddha: Buddhist Civilization in India and Ceylon*. London: Temple Smith, 1973.

Gurinder Singh Mann, Paul David Numrich, and Raymond B. Williams, *Buddhists, Hindus, and Sikhs in America*. New York: Oxford University Press, 2001.

David S. Noss and John B. Noss, *A History of the World's Religions*. New York: Macmillan, 1990.

Daniel L. Overmyer, *Religions of China: The World as a Living System*. San Francisco: HarperSanFrancisco, 1986.

Diana Paul, *Women in Buddhism*. Berkeley, CA: Asian Humanities, 1980.

Charles S. Prebish, *American Buddhism.* Belmont, CA: Wadsworth, 1979.

Richard H. Robinson and Willard L. Johnson, *The Buddhist Religion: A Historical Introduction.* Belmont, CA: Wadsworth, 1982.

Shih Pao-ch'ang, *Lives of the Nuns: Biographies of Chinese Buddhist Nuns from the Fourth to Sixth Centuries.* Trans. Kathryn Ann Tsai. Honolulu: University of Hawaii Press, 1994.

David L. Snellgrave, *The Image of the Buddha.* Tokyo: Kodansha International, 1978.

D.T. Suzuki, *Essays in Zen Buddhism.* London: Rider, 1953.

Donald Swearer, *Secrets of the Lotus.* New York: Macmillan, 1971.

Thich Nhat Hanh, *Vietnam: Lotus in a Sea of Fire.* New York: Hill and Wang, 1967.

————, *Zen Keys: A Zen Monk Examines the Vietnamese Tradition.* New York: Anchor, 1974.

E.J. Thomas, *The Life of the Buddha as Legend and History.* London: Routledge and Kegan Paul, 1927.

Laurence G. Thompson, *Chinese Religion: An Introduction.* Belmont, CA: Wadsworth, 1980.

John Walters, *The Essence of Buddhism.* New York: Thomas Y. Crowell, 1961.

Henry C. Warren, ed., *Buddhism in Translations.* New York: Atheneum, 1963.

Burton Watson, trans., *The Lotus Sutra.* New York: Columbia University Press, 1993.

Alan Watts, *Buddhism, the Religion of No-Religion.* Boston: Charles E. Tuttle, 1996.

————, *The Way of Zen.* New York: Vintage, 1957.

————, *What Is Zen?* Novato, CA: New World Library, 2000.

Stanley Wolpert, *A New History of India.* 7th ed. New York: Oxford University Press, 2004.

Periodicals

Graham Christian, "Going Buddhist: Panic and Emptiness, the Buddha and Me," *Library Journal*, January 2005.

Peter N. Gregor, "Describing the Elephant: Buddhism in America," *Religion and American Culture*, vol. 11, 2001.

John Makransky, "Buddhist Perspectives on Truth in Other Religions: Past and Present," *Theological Studies*, June 2003.

Seth Mydans, "An Ex-telemarketer's Other Life as a Buddhist Saint," *New York Times*, June 12, 2004.

Noelle Oxenhalter, "Money and the Middle Way," *Utne Reader*, September/October 2004.

Donald K. Swearer, "Three Modes of Zen Buddhism in America," *Journal of Ecumenical Studies*, vol. 10, 1973.

Web Sites

About Buddhism, www.aboutbuddhism.org. This is an easy to use Web site focusing on Tibetan Buddhism but also providing general articles on basic Buddhist history and beliefs.

Buddhanet, www.buddhanet.net. This Web site provides a comprehensive overview of Buddhism around the world. Managed by the Buddha Dharma Education Association, the site contains articles, links, multimedia, ebooks, and other resources.

DharmaNet International, www.dharmanet.org. This Web site provides general information on Buddhism, resources for further study, databases, and chat rooms.

Fundamental Buddhism Explained, www.fundamentalbuddhism.com. This Web site is run by the Buddhist Instruction Ministry. It seeks to explain Buddhism based on a close reading of the original Buddha's teachings.

Index